PUBLIC AND PRIVATE PENSIONS IN CANADA:
AN ECONOMIC ANALYSIS

J. E. Pesando and S. A. Rea jr

Public and Private Pensions in Canada: an economic analysis

PUBLISHED FOR THE ONTARIO ECONOMIC COUNCIL BY
UNIVERSITY OF TORONTO PRESS
TORONTO AND BUFFALO

Canadian Cataloguing in Publication Data

Pesando, James E., 1946-
  Public and private pensions in Canada

  (Ontario Economic Council research studies; 9)

  Bibliography: p.
  ISBN 0-8020-3347-4

  1. Old age pensions – Canada. I. Rea, Samuel A.,
  1944- II. Title. III. Series: Ontario Economic
  Council. Ontario Economic Council research
  studies; 9.

  HD7106.C2P48   331.2'52'0971   C77-001302-3

This study reflects the views of the authors and not necessarily those of the
Ontario Economic Council.

This book has been published during the
Sesquicentennial year of the University of Toronto.

Contents

Acknowledgments

The authors wish to thank Richard Bird, Yehuda Kotowitz, Constantine Kapsalis, and J. Wells Bentley for their helpful comments at various stages of the preparation of this report. Only the authors, of course, assume responsibility for the views expressed in the report. Les Cseh's programming effort made the CPP simulation possible. Susan Moses and Sharon Bolt deserve special thanks for their patience in typing and retyping the manuscript. This book is based on a report 'Retirement Incomes and Public Policy,' submitted to the Ontario Economic Council in September 1976.

PUBLIC AND PRIVATE PENSIONS IN CANADA:
AN ECONOMIC ANALYSIS

1
Introduction

The adequacy of both public and private pension schemes has become a topic of increasing concern in recent years. With regard to the Canada Pension Plan (CPP), for example, a number of important issues have surfaced. Can the CPP continue to pay benefits according to its present formula without an increase in contribution rates? Does the CPP as currently structured provide disproportionate benefits to certain income classes and/or age cohorts? Are the problems anticipated for the CPP exacerbated by demographic trends, including the significant aging of the population foreseen in the years ahead? The recent increase in the rate of inflation has focused attention on a crucial problem facing private pension plans. Can private pensions provide for the full indexation of benefits with respect to inflation, as do the CPP and the superannuation plan for federal civil servants, and yet remain actuarially sound? The importance of this question is hard to overemphasize. With inflation at 10 per cent a year, for example, the real value of a fixed dollar pension will have fallen to 39 per cent of its original value after only ten years.

The purpose of this monograph is to analyse several of these and other important issues. The prime focus is on the evaluation of government policies which concern, either directly or indirectly, the provision of retirement incomes. Both the federal and provincial governments exert an important impact in this area. The several provincial Pension Benefits Acts contain most of the regulations which govern the operations of private pension plans. The federal government administers the Canada Pension Plan together with the Old Age Security and Guaranteed Income Supplement programs. The Province of Ontario has its own supplementary programs, the Guaranteed Annual Income System and the Ontario Tax Credit, both of which provide income for the aged. The monograph examines the policies of both the federal government and of the Province of Ontario. The analysis of the federal programs is conducted from the perspective of a resident of Ontario, and thus involves the joint treatment of certain federal and Ontario programs together with tax provisions relevant to an Ontario resident.

The analysis in the monograph is divided into two parts: the first deals with private pension plans; the second, with public programs that provide retirement incomes. More than forty per cent of the labour force in Canada now belong to private pension plans which, by virtue of their additional flexibility, serve to complement public programs in this area. The evolution of these plans is governed in large part by the provincial regulatory authorities together with the relevant tax provisions of the Department of National Revenue.

The concern in chapter two is with certain provincial regulations dealing with the vesting and 'locking-in' of pension benefits. At present, minimum vesting provisions contained in Ontario's Pension Benefits Act and its counterparts require only that pension benefits vest (i.e. the employee becomes entitled to contributions made by the employer on his behalf) after the employee has attained age 45 *and* completed ten years of service. Further, current regulations provide that both employee and employer contributions to a private pension plan be "locked in", that is the employee cannot opt for a cash withdrawal of either his own or his employer's contributions on his behalf, but must take his (vested) benefits in the form of a deferred pension. The recognition that pension benefits represent a form of deferred wages, the viewpoint adopted in this report, provides an important perspective on proposed revisions to statutory vesting and 'locking-in' provisions. The discussion of these issues focuses attention on the age discriminatory features of most formula pension plans, a fact which does not appear to be well understood by the public at large.

The recent escalation in the rate of inflation in Canada serves to highlight perhaps the major limitation of the private pension system: its apparent inability to provide adequate retirement incomes in an inflationary climate. The problems posed by inflation for private pension plans are discussed at length in chapters three and four. For organizational purposes, these problems are divided into those pertaining to the pre-retirement years and those pertaining to the post-retirement years. Final earnings plans, in which the pension of the employee is geared to his income just prior to his retirement, serve to insulate the pension benefits of the employee from inflation which occurs during his work years. This result reflects the fact that the wages of a typical employee will rise in tandem with inflation, in addition to incorporating increases in productivity. Final earnings plans are far from universal, however, and those plans which do exist have experienced large actuarial deficiencies during the recent period of escalating inflation. More importantly, private pensions plans – unlike (for example) the Canada Pension Plan – do not provide for the indexation of pension benefits during the employee's retirement years. At present, the attempt by private pension plans to provide relief to pensioners is largely confined to ad hoc adjustments which serve, at best, to compensate only partially for the erosion of fixed-dollar benefits by inflation. A central question is whether private pension plans could provide for the indexation of pension benefits after retirement and yet remain actuarially sound.

The most important of the public programs are the Canada Pension Plan (CPP), Old Age Security (OAS), Guaranteed Income Supplement (GIS), and Guaranteed Annual Income System (GAINS). These programs are briefly reviewed in chapter five. In general, government programs that provide retirement incomes appear to have at least four primary objectives: (1) to provide an income for the aged with minimal alternative means of support; (2) to pass on some of the current increases in real income to older members of society; (3) to provide for means by which individuals (or their employers) can save for their own retirement income; and (4) to ensure that the public or private plans do not overly distort the individual's incentives to work and save. These objectives provide the conceptual framework in which both the present public programs and proposed changes to these programs are analyzed and evaluated.

The concern of chapter six is with the method of financing public pension programs. At the extremes, the choice is between a pay-as-you-go system, which finances current benefits with current taxes or contributions, and an investment fund system, which finances current benefits from an investment fund created with contributions made in the past. In the investment fund approach, current contributions are sufficient to cover *fully* on an actuarial basis the future pension benefits generated by those contributions. A public pension program may, in fact, be funded by a combination of these two techniques. The choice of the method of financing must be made regardless of whether or not the public program is financed with contributions. In chapter six, however, this choice is analysed only in the context of the CPP. The choice of the method of financing also has important redistributive effects, primarily between generations. A pay-as-you-go system, for example, will clearly favour those who are retired when the system is introduced. The financing decision is also related to another potential problem, the rising percentage of the population that are past retirement age. If the recent slowdown in population growth persists, the ratio of the retired population to the working population must increase. Concern has been expressed that this development will place an excessive burden on workers who must support the retired population. The choice of the optimal method of financing, as amplified in the text, is directly related to the ratio of retired to active workers.

Another issue of central importance is the extent to which the present public programs redistribute income. This issue, which has several dimensions, is analysed in chapter seven. At one point in time, these programs would appear to benefit older at the expense of younger people. Do they at the same time, however, redistribute income between income classes? Since the young will eventually become beneficiaries of these programs, what is the extent of redistribution over a lifetime? These issues are of particular importance for the Canada Pension Plan, where the extent to which benefits are related to contributions is a topic of general concern. The extent to which the CPP redistributes income to particular income classes or to particular demographic groups has an important bearing on proposed modifications of the system. The suggestion has been made, for example, that housewives should be incorporated into the CPP system. This proposal, depending on how it is formulated, might have substantial redistributive effects. Another change to be considered is the inevitable increase in CPP contribution rates. The redistributive implications of this modification need to be examined in a lifetime context.

The public programs which transfer income to the aged are likely to influence individual behaviour. These incentive effects are examined in chapter eight. The implicit tax on private income may discourage work and also discourage private saving. A reduction in private saving could also result because the public programs are substitutes for private pension plans. If this response is significant, the capital stock in the economy could be reduced, depending on the method of financing.

PRIVATE PENSION PLANS

2
Vesting, portability, and locking-in

INTRODUCTION: PENSION BENEFITS AS DEFERRED WAGES

A major objective of Ontario's Pension Benefits Act of 1965 is to minimize the
loss of pension rights when employees change jobs, by explicitly setting forth
regulations concerning the vesting and portability of pension benefits. Vesting
refers to the employee's right to all or part of the *employer* contributions made
on his behalf upon termination of employment prior to retirement. At present,
the Act specifies that a pension plan member who leaves employment after
reaching age 45 *and* after completing ten years of service is entitled to a deferred
pension equal to his earned pension under the terms of the plan. Further,
benefits which vest are 'locked-in,' since the terminating employee is *not* allowed
to withdraw either his contributions or the contributions paid by the employer
on his behalf. The Act thus seeks to ensure that vested benefits are taken in the
form of a deferred pension rather than in the form of an immediate cash
settlement.[1]

The adequacy of statutory vesting and 'locking-in' provisions remains,
however, the subject of considerable controversy. Many observers, recognizing
that pension benefits represent a form of deferred wages, argue that the '45 and

---

1 Two exceptions exist under the Act with respect to the locking-in of vested pension
benefits. First, where the deferred life annuity or the pension benefit is less than $10
per month, the value of the annuity or benefit may be commuted (converted to cash).
Second, a private pension plan may provide for an employee who terminates prior to his
retirement to receive, in partial discharge of his rights under the plan, a lump sum up to
a maximum of 25 per cent of the commuted value of the deferred life annuity.

10' rule be replaced by immediate vesting. In its submission to the first annual meeting of the Canadian Association of Pension Supervisory Authorities, the Canadian Labour Congress (1975, 6-7) notes: 'If the principle of deferred wages is to have a practical meaning in the realm of private pensions, improvement of the vesting provisions must be the first priority ... While the principle suggests that there should be full and immediate vesting of all benefits, practice might prove difficult.'

The purpose of this chapter is to analyse the implications for vesting and 'locking-in' which stem from the recognition that pension benefits represent a form of deferred wages. In so doing, the analysis seeks to clarify a number of issues which do not appear to be well understood. To what extent, for example, does an employee forfeit income – in the form of a claim to employer contributions on his behalf – if his pension benefits fail to vest? To what extent would a change to immediate vesting be accompanied by a change in effective wage grids so as to greater reward length of service and thus provide employers an alternative means of retaining skilled workers and reducing turnover? Indeed, to what extent is the concern expressed by the Canadian Labour Congress and other observers regarding the adequacy of vesting and 'locking-in' provisions really justified? These issues receive considerable attention in later sections of this chapter, but must be preceded by a more detailed statement of why pension benefits must be viewed as a form of deferred wages.

To some, the argument that pension benefits represent a form of deferred wages is self-apparent; to others (Asimakopulos and Weldon (1970)), this argument is at odds with the view that private pension plans have an important 'familial' element and/or reflect the paternalism and benevolence of the employer. Most observers (US Congress, 1973) argue that pensions *today* are best viewed as a form of deferred compensation. To the extent that labour negotiators are willing to trade off current wages for higher pension benefits, the deferred wage interpretation is obviously supported. In a recent study of 33,000 workers in 133 large firms in the United States, Schiller and Weiss (1977) provide evidence that, *ceteris paribus,* current wages are lower, the larger are the pension benefits to which the workers are entitled.

The argument that pension benefits are a form of deferred wages has, however, more subtle dimensions. Consider, for example, ad hoc adjustments to pensions in force made unilaterally by some Canadian firms in recent years to help preserve the real pension benefits of retired employees. Superficially, such adjustments may appear to contradict the view that pension benefits represent deferred wages. Such benefits, for which the employer is not contractually liable, cannot be directly linked to the earlier provision of labour services. These ad hoc adjustments may, however, represent the honouring by the employer of an implicit contract with his employees in which he undertakes to reduce the income risk of the employees. Income risk refers to the fact that the wages of the employee – current or deferred – are likely to represent his major source of income and hence render him vulnerable to their interruption or erosion. This interpretation is in the spirit of recent work by Gordon (1974) and Azariadis (1975).[2] Less formally, by honouring an unenforceable but implicit obligation to its employees, the firm maintains the reputation of being a 'good' employer which, *ceteris paribus,* permits it to hire workers at a lower total wage, including both current and deferred components, than would an alternative firm which either did not provide or did not honour similar implicit agreements. Consider, as an additional example, the situation in which a union negotiates improved pension benefits for *both* employed and retired workers. In effect, the union may be viewed as accepting a smaller compensation package for its workers than might otherwise be the case on the implicit assumption that, in the future, these workers will receive similar consideration during their retirement years. The expectation that the union in succeeding periods will protect future retirees is similar in kind to the expectation that successor governments will honour the commitments contained in today's public pension programs.

The alternative to viewing pensions as a form of deferred wages is to view them as the byproduct of employer benevolence and/or 'familial' ties between the employer and (long-term) employees. This alternative viewpoint is, in the opinion of the authors, not sustainable.[3] As noted in an earlier example, apparent acts of employer benevolence may be given an interpretation consistent with the view that pensions represent deferred wages. Similarly, the argument that employers use their pension plans as a means of 'rewarding' long-term employees may be given an economic explanation in terms of optimizing behaviour. In particular, employers may be regarded as seeking – to the extent that they are able – to defer wages in such a fashion as to minimize employee turnover and thus to retain skilled employees.

This chapter thus adopts the view that pension benefits, to the extent that they reflect employer contributions, are a form of deferred wages. It begins with a brief review designed to provide a historical perspective on current vesting and

2 The implicit contract argument would appear to be particularly relevant in the context of ad hoc adjustments for inflation, since the initial benefits would presumably have been viewed by both parties as denominated in real terms.

3 Formal discrimination between the 'implicit contract' and 'benevolence' theories of pension benefits would first require differences in the comparative static predictions of the two theories. Loosely, the 'implicit contract' theory would imply that companies *which hire from the same labour pool and which have roughly similar compensation packages* would be likely to follow the lead if one of their number were to unilaterally improve benefits and make the improvements retroactive. The 'benevolence' theory would appear to have no such implication.

'locking-in' provisions, followed by two sections which treat, in some detail, the economics of vesting and 'locking-in.' The perspective on statutory vesting and 'locking-in' provisions implied by the earlier analysis is then presented. An analysis of the proposed liberalization of the statutory vesting rule to age 40 and five years of service completes the main body of the chapter.

VESTING AND 'LOCKING-IN': AN HISTORICAL PERSPECTIVE

Surveys conducted by Statistics Canada (1972) indicate that in 1965 (i.e., prior to the enactment of the Pension Benefits Act of Ontario) more than 96 per cent of all private pension plans in Canada provided for some form of vesting. This result reflects the Department of National Revenue's requirement that private pension plans provide for vesting conditions not to exceed the attainment of age 50 and 20 years of service or participation in order to qualify for registration and hence favourable tax treatment. Employees, however, could – and usually did – opt to forfeit the vested benefit in order to obtain a refund of their own contributions. The study conducted by Statistics Canada in 1965 indicated that only 3 per cent of the 243,000 plan members who terminated their employment during that year became entitled to a deferred pension, while the great majority received the return of their own contributions only.

Ontario's Pension Benefits Act of 1965, together with parallel legislation in Alberta, Quebec, Saskatchewan, the Northwest Territories and Yukon Territory, was designed in large part both to liberalize vesting requirements and to ensure that vested benefits took the form of deferred annuities. The Act provides for the vesting of employer contributions after the employee has attained age 45 and completed ten years of service. The Act further provides that employer contributions together with the employee's own contributions on his behalf must be 'locked-in' to provide the plan member with a deferred pension to commence at normal retirement age under the plan.

The Act and its counterparts throughout Canada served as a major impetus to the liberalization of vesting rights. All plans were required as a minimum to adopt the '45 and 10' rule, although many plans contained more liberal vesting provisions. In both Canada and the United States, even in the absence of legislation, the trend in recent years has been toward less restrictive vesting provisions.[4] The movement toward the liberalization of vesting provisions in Canada is evident in the data (Canada, 1972a) compiled by Statistics Canada

---

4 For the US experience, see Bankers Trust Company (1975). The trend in the United States has been away from vesting after an age and service requirement, and toward vesting after a period of service only.

regarding vesting regulations in private pension plans in the years 1965 and 1970. Two results in particular are worth noting. First, the most significant impact of the revised legislative environment would appear to be the dramatic reduction in the number of members in plans which had no vesting provisions at all. The number of members in such plans declined from 516,610 in 1965 to 68,020 in 1970. These figures represent 22 per cent and 3 per cent of the total plan membership in 1965 and 1970, respectively. Second, vesting requirements continue to be liberalized beyond the minimum standards prescribed by the new legislation. The proportion of plan members who are subject to vesting requirements of 10 years or less of service or participation, for example, increased from 29.8 per cent in 1965 to 45.3 per cent in 1970.

The *motivation* for the 'locking-in' of vested benefits appears to stem from the fact that prior to the enactment of such provisions, the majority of employees who terminated prior to retirement received only the return of their own contributions. Most private pension plans permitted terminating employees to obtain a refund of their own contributions in return for the forfeiture of the vested pension. The result was that the majority of employees elected to receive a cash refund, thus forgoing their claim to employers' contributions made on their behalf. Concern with this situation is evident in the study by the Ontario Committee on Portable Pensions (Ontario, 1961). The Committee compiled data pertaining to the percentage of Government of Canada employees who terminated after having met the minimum vesting requirement (five years service) under the Public Service Superannuation Act prior to December 1957. The vast majority, for all age groups, elected cash withdrawal and thus forfeited their claim to the government's contributions on their behalf. Of males age 25, for example, 92.8 per cent elected cash withdrawal. This percentage declined steadily, but only modestly, with age. Of males age 58, the oldest age for which data are presented, 67.4 per cent still elected cash withdrawal and hence forfeited their vested benefits. Two points merit emphasis. First, older employees elected cash withdrawal less frequently, a rational response in view of the fact (discussed later) that the value of vested benefits is likely to be smaller for younger than for older employees. Second, a significant majority of older employees nonetheless elected cash withdrawal, in spite of the fact that the value of the forfeited vested benefits could be quite large.

THE ECONOMICS OF VESTING

The fact that pension benefits are deferred wages provides, at least on the surface, support for the argument that vesting ought to be full and immediate. If such is not the case, the employee who receives a portion of his wages in the form of employer contributions toward the purchase of a deferred pension is subject to the risk that he will forfeit these wages by leaving his job before meeting the vesting requirements. If his benefits have not vested, an employee will receive only the return of his contributions plus interest, but not the contributions made by the employer on his behalf. The purpose of statutory vesting requirements is to protect employees from the loss of pension benefits when they change jobs. To the extent that employers use delayed vesting to discourage turnover and to retain skilled workers, however, its elimination is likely to result in effective wage grids which are more steeply graded with respect to length of service. This point merits additional comment.

Delayed vesting may be used by an employer as a substitute for wage scales which rise more steeply with years of service, seniority-linked promotions and vacation pay, and so forth. A firm may be willing, for example, to pay for training and experience which produces *general* skills (i.e., skills which increase the productivity of the worker in other firms by as much as in the firm which provides the training) if delayed vesting ensures that the trained employee has a strong incentive to remain with the firm. If delayed vesting is prohibited by law, the cost of this training or experience is likely to be passed to the employee in the form of lower wages during his initial period of employment. To the extent that capital markets are imperfect, or to the extent that the employee cannot borrow against his future earnings to finance this training or experience, the elimination of delayed vesting could serve as a disincentive to the investment in human capital.

Delayed vesting, in addition, may be viewed as a type of insurance (Becker, 1964) for firms which share with the employee the cost of *specific* training or experience (i.e., training or experience which increases the productivity of labour by more in the firm which provides the training or experience than in other firms). In effect, the firm receives as a lump-sum payment the non-vested contributions of a terminating employee as compensation for its share of the cost of the training or experience provided to the employee. The elimination of delayed vesting would encourage employers, *ceteris paribus,* to transfer this cost to the employee. As a result, the effective wage grid faced by the employee would be steeped more sharply with respect to years of service. If the employee were to change jobs, he would face the prospect of a loss in terms of the foregone return on his investment. Under the present system, he loses non-vested pension benefits.

The elimination of delayed vesting is thus likely to be accompanied, at least to some extent, by compensatory changes in effective wage grids. Pay scales are likely to become more steeply graded with respect to years of service and/or fringe benefits linked to seniority are likely to increase as firms seek an alternative way to minimize employee turnover and retain skilled employees. Proponents of immediate vesting appear to have two objectives: first, to prevent the loss of employee benefits (deferred wages) when an employee changes jobs, a loss which may be substantial in view of the discontinuities inherent in present vesting requirements; and second, to ensure that decisions by the employee with regard to job selection are not overly complicated by the need to assess the value of the benefits which he would forfeit if he switches jobs. To the extent that compensatory changes in effective wage grids occur, the first goal will be (at least) partially thwarted. Wage grids which rise more steeply with respect to years of service impose a cost on employees who switch jobs not dissimilar, except for the abruptness of the discontinuities, to cost imposed by vesting requirements. To the extent that these compensatory changes occur, the benefits of immediate vesting in terms of reducing the loss in (deferred) wages which occurs when an employee switches jobs may be illusory. To the extent that such changes do *not* occur, the employee may benefit in the manner intended by those who advocate the elimination of deferred vesting.

If the move to immediate vesting were to take place and if compensatory changes in wage grids were not to occur, the gain to the employee would depend primarily on the type of plan in which he is a member. Private pension plans may be grouped into three major classifications: (1) *unit benefit plans,* under which pension benefits are determined with reference to remuneration of any employee for each year or for a selected number of years of service; (2) *flat benefit plans,* under which pension benefits are expressed either as a fixed amount in respect of each year of employment or as a fixed periodic amount; and (3) *money purchase plans,* under which pension benefits are determined upon the retirement of an employee with reference to the accumulated amount of or the total contributions paid by or for the credit of the employee. The first two types of plans are examples of *defined benefit plans,* while the third is an example of a *defined contribution plan.* Defined benefit plans are either contributory, in which both the employee and the employer make contributions on the employee's behalf, or non-contributory, in which only the employer makes contributions.[5]

In the case of money purchase plans or non-contributory defined benefit plans, the loss to the employee if he leaves his job before his benefits have vested is easy to calculate. For the money purchase plan, the loss is equal to the

5 The fact that certain plans are non-contributory, or that employees do not make payments from their current wages into the plan, does not imply that the employer assumes the entire cost of the pension plan. One need simply note that the higher 'fringe' benefits in the form of a non-contributory plan are likely to be reflected *ceteris paribus* in lower current wages.

accumulated value of the employer's contributions, as the employee is entitled to the return of only the accumulated value of his own contributions. For the non-contributory defined benefit plan, the loss is equal to the capital sum necessary to purchase the pension benefits to which the employee's service record would have entitled him if he had met the vesting requirements. The calculation of the loss to the employee if he is a member of a contributory defined benefit plan is more complex. The employer's contribution to which the employee becomes entitled if his benefits vest, equals the actuarial value of the deferred pension, less the accumulated value of the employee's own contributions. For certain types of contributory defined benefit plans, the young employee bears almost the entire cost of his pension, and hence the benefit to him of earlier or immediate vesting may be close to zero.

This important point is illustrated in Table 1 with an example drawn from the Ontario Committee (Ontario, 1961). The salient details of a representative unit benefit plan are listed together with a table depicting, under single premium funding,[6] the cost to both the employer and the employee of purchasing the indicated pension benefits at different ages of the employee. When the employee is age 25, for example, his annual contribution of $250.00 (5 per cent of earnings) is sufficient to purchase the entire pension benefit to which he becomes entitled during that year. By the time the employee reaches age 45, a contribution by the employer almost equal to the annual contribution of the employee is necessary to purchase the pension benefit to which the employee becomes entitled in that year. Finally, as the employee approaches retirement age under the plan, the contribution required from the employer to purchase the pension benefit in that year is several times the annual contribution of the employee. The higher contribution required of the employer as the age of the employee increases reflects two factors: (1) the younger the employee, the longer will be the period in which his own contributions earn interest, and (2) the younger the employee, the greater is the probability that he will die or leave the plan without qualifying for full pension benefits.

The recognition that the cost to the employer will, for a large variety of plans, increase with the age of the employee is widespread (US Congress, 1973, Ontario, 1961). For a defined benefit plan in which all years of service count

---

6 Under *single premium funding,* the pension benefit earned or accrued for each year of plan membership is bought or funded in that year. This method contrasts with *level premium funding,* in which a constant annual premium (expressed in dollars per employee or as a percentage of payroll) is determined so as to provide for all future benefits. In general, the cost for an individual tends to be higher when he is young and lower when he is old in the case of level premium relative to single premium funding.

TABLE 1

The impact of employee age on employer contributions for a representative private pension plan

Age attained	(1) Worker's contribution ($)	Men (2) Employer's contribution ($)	Men (3) Combined annual contribution ($)	Women (4) Employer's contribution ($)	Women (5) Combined annual contribution ($)
25	250	0	250	0	250
30	250	15	265	53	303
35	250	73	323	119	369
40	250	143	393	199	449
45	250	228	478	296	546
50	250	332	582	415	665
55	250	458	708	559	809
60	250	611	861	734	984
64	250	757	1007	901	1151

SOURCE: Ontario (1961, 29)

NOTES: Analysis assumes: (1) *retirement* at age 65; (2) *assumed earnings* of $5000 per year at all ages; (3) *pension* equal to 2 per cent of earnings for each year of service; (4) *vesting* is full and immediate; (5) *death benefit* consists of refund of employee contributions with 4 per cent interest; (6) *employee contribution*: 5 per cent of earnings, *employer contribution*: the required balance as shown above; (7) *interest rate* of 4 per cent equally in determining the pension benefit, the key determinant of whether or not the cost to the employer rises or falls with the age of the employee is the relationship between the rate of interest and the rate of growth of employee earnings. For simplicity, assume that it is known with certainty that the employee will remain with the firm and live to retirement age. Consider the case of an employee who enters a defined benefit plan at age 40 and who retires at age 65. The value at age 65 of the employee's contribution at age 40, twenty-five years earlier, will be $KW_o (1 + r)^{25}$ where K is the fraction of his earnings which he contributes to the plan, W_o is his salary at age 40, and r is the rate of interest earned by the plan. The value at age 65 of an employee's contribution at age 41, twenty-four years earlier, will be $KW_o (1 + g) (1 + r)^{24}$ where g is the rate of growth of his earnings. When the employee reaches age 65, the employer must pay the difference between the cumulated value of the employee's contribution and the capital sum necessary to purchase the annuity which corresponds to the promised pension benefits. So long as the value of the pension to which the employee becomes entitled for each year of service is the same, the *employer's* cost will be greater when the employee is older — 41 rather than 40 — if $KW_o (1 + g) (1 + r)^{24}$ is less than $KW_o (1 + r)^{25}$; that is, if the rate of interest (r) is greater than the rate of growth of wages (g). In the illustration in Table 1, for example, the rate of interest (4 per cent) exceeds the rate of growth of earnings (zero per cent) and hence the cost to the employer increases with the age of the employee. In fact, a younger employee is less likely to become eligible for his pension than an older employee because of the greater likelihood that he will terminate employment or die before he reaches retirement age under the plan. Thus the employer's costs will increase with the age of the employee if, for example, the rate of interest equals or only modestly exceeds the rate of growth of earnings. Significantly, tax regulations of the Department of National Revenue (see chapter three) require that pension plans be costed with the assumption that the rate of interest exceed the rate of growth of earnings, usually by at least one per cent. To the extent that this regulation is consistent with actual experience, employer's costs will increase as the employee increases in age. If the plan is actuarially sound, the result must be that the employee pays most of the cost of the pension to which he becomes entitled during his younger years. If the regulation is not consistent with actual experience, then two things will occur. First, the plan will continually experience actuarial deficits, with the employer (presumably) assuming the additional cost. Second, the cost to the employer *may* no longer increase with the age of the employee, although (clearly) his total costs will be higher. The evidence presented in chapter three suggests that the requirement that the rate of interest exceed the rate of growth of earnings by one per cent can be achieved, in the aggregate, only if (1) the plan is heavily invested in common stocks and (2) the real return on common stocks remains in line with historical experience.

The argument that vesting ought to be both full and immediate thus requires two further qualifications. First, with the exception of money purchase and non-contributory defined benefit plans, the employee may pay most of the cost of his accrued pension benefits during his early working years. In 1970, 78 per cent of all plan members were in contributory plans while more than 90 per cent were in defined benefit plans (Canada, 1972a). As a result, liberalization of vesting provisions to permit benefits to vest at an earlier age than (say) 40 may be largely illusory since the employers' contributions to which the employee becomes entitled (i.e., the actuarial value of the deferred pension less the accumulated value of the employee's own contributions) may be minimal. Second, to the extent that vesting is accompanied by the 'locking-in' of *both* employee and employer contributions, earlier vesting may simply amount to the 'locking-in' of the employee's own contributions. If the rate of return on the savings represented by the employee's own contributions is low relative to the return on alternative forms of savings, the employee may actually lose if vesting provisions are liberalized. In view of the avowed purpose of the Pension Benefits Act to better inform employees of their pension rights, one can construct a persuasive case for requiring that the guarantor of each plan indicate, at different employee ages, the approximate division of the costs of the pension benefits between the employer and the employee.

THE ECONOMICS OF 'LOCKING-IN'

The Pension Benefits Act of Ontario requires that benefits which vest be 'locked-in'; that is, the terminating employee is not allowed to withdraw either his contributions or the contributions paid by the employer on his behalf. As currently constituted, the 'locking-in' provisions have two principal effects: first, they ensure that the terminating employee cannot forfeit his share of employer contributions; and second, in so doing, they ensure that the accumulated savings of the terminating employee in the form of his claim to a deferred pension are used to provide a retirement income rather than (say) to finance an increase in current consumption.

The first effect reflects the paternalistic nature of these provisions, as the legislation is clearly designed to protect the employee from acting against the legislator's perception of the employee's self-interest. The evidence concerning the voluntary forfeiture of the claim to employer contributions was clearly of great concern to those responsible for the drafting of pension legislation. Although the current 'locking-in' provisions accomplish this objective, alternatives do exist. The pension legislation, for example, could permit a terminating employee to withdraw his own contributions, yet not forfeit his claim to employer contributions on his behalf. Recent United States legislation in the pension field has moved in this direction (US Congress, 1974).

In short, the 'locking-in' provision as currently enacted could be relaxed considerably if its purpose were only to protect the employee's claim to vested pension benefits. Because the protection of an employee's vested benefits could be accomplished without requiring the 'locking-in' of his own contributions, the second effect of these provisions is accentuated. This effect refers to the 'forced' saving imposed on the terminating employee by virtue of the fact that he cannot draw upon the accumulated value even of his own contributions in order to finance current consumption. The legislative provisions thus impinge upon the consumption-savings decision of the terminating employee in order to ensure that the accumulated savings implicit in his claim to a deferred pension are used to provide retirement income. The economic rationale behind the restriction of individual discretion in this area lies in the external costs imposed on society as a whole if an individual does not adequately provide for his own retirement income. Each retiree represents an (actuarial) claim on income-related supplementary pension programs of both the Federal and Provincial governments. To the extent that an individual opts for high consumption during his work years, the size of the actuarial claim on general tax revenues increases. If an individual fails to accumulate sufficient savings to provide an adequate income for himself during his retirement years, taxpayers as a whole will effectively subsidize his retirement income.

This externality argument, however, has been weakened by the introduction of the Canada Pension Plan. The existence of this plan, in which the worker's benefits vest immediately and are completely 'locked-in,' reduces – but does not eliminate – the probability that a terminating employee who opts for cash withdrawal will ultimately draw benefits from an income-related public pension program. One might seek to justify the 'locking-in' provisions on the grounds that they represent the 'price' that employees must pay in order to avail themselves of the tax deductability status of pension contributions. This argument, however, is invalidated by the existence of Registered Retirement Savings Plans (RRSPs) as an alternative (or complementary) vehicle with which to provide for retirement income. RRSPs are, in effect, money purchase plans into which only the individual makes contributions. The maximum annual contribution is the lesser of $4000 or 20 per cent of earned income if the individual is not a member of an employer-sponsored private pension plan. These contributions are tax deductible, yet the savings which accumulate in the RRSP are 'locked-in' only to the extent that tax incentives discourage the individual from liquidating the RRSP prior to retirement. If an individual liquidates a RRSP prior to retirement, *ceteris paribus* his lifetime taxes are likely to increase. This increase in his tax burden, in turn, may be viewed as a partial (at least) internalization of the externality corresponding to the increase in the likelihood of his making a claim on income-related public pension programs. In a directly analogous fashion, one can argue that benefits which vest in a private pension plan should be 'locked-in' only by the same tax incentives which discourage liquidation of a RRSP.

Given the legislative concern with ensuring that the accumulated savings implicit in the vested benefit are not used to finance current consumption, there still remains the issue of whether or not the forced choice of the *savings vehicle* can also be justified. The legislation clearly dictates not only that the terminating employee must save rather than consume, but also that he save in the form of a claim to a deferred annuity. This second constraint invites the concern, resurrected repeatedly in the current inflationary climate, of whether the implicit return to savings in this form is (1) low relative to alternative investment vehicles and (2) inadequate in terms of providing a positive real return in an inflationary climate. The analysis in chapter three suggests that this concern is justified.

Finally, the issue of the joint revision in both 'locking-in' and vesting provisions merits comment. If vesting provisions are liberalized, the issue of whether or not the current 'locking-in' provisions should apply will logically be raised. The Ontario Committee on Portable Pensions, for example, not only recommended graduated vesting commencing at age 30, but also that restrictions on cash withdrawal of employer contributions should apply at the same age at which the vesting of pension benefits begins. In its 'Green Paper' issued in 1972, the Ontario Pension Commission appears to suggest that the 'locking-in' of both employee and employer contributions would occur simultaneously with the vesting of benefits under the proposed '40 and 5' rule as under the current '45 and 10.'

The central issue is whether or not the employee is really better off with a more relaxed vesting requirement if such a relaxation also entails the 'locking-in' of his own contributions as well. An employee whose benefits vest at an earlier age as a result of an amendment to the Pension Benefits Act, and whose contributions together with those of his employer are accordingly 'locked-in,' may actually be worse off than if no change in the statutory vesting requirements were made. The 'locked-in' contributions may consist almost entirely of funds that he has contributed from his current wages, on which he will now earn a lower rate of return than would be available on alternative savings vehicles. Except for employees in defined contribution (money purchase) or non-contributory defined benefit plans, the advantage to the employee of requiring that pension benefits vest at an earlier age may be largely illusory.

VESTING AND 'LOCKING-IN': THE RRSP ALTERNATIVE

A useful question to ask is whether or not an employee would be better off if (1) he saved for his retirement through membership in an employer pension plan or (2) he received his *full* wages, *including the actuarial equivalent of the employer contributions to the private pension plan,* and saved for his retirement in the form of a RRSP. The advantages of the RRSP are readily apparent: vesting would be full and immediate; contributions to the RRSP would be 'locked-in' only to the extent that tax incentives discourage liquidation of the RRSP during the high-income work years; and the returns earned on the savings would be commensurate with market yields.

An additional issue, however, is whether the maximum permissible pension is greater under (1) a private pension plan or (2) a RRSP. DNR Information Circular 72-13R3, dated 1 December 1975, indicates that the maximum pension payable under a private pension plan cannot exceed $1143 times the number of years of service not exceeding 35, or a maximum pension of $40,000 per year (paragraph 9(g)). The corresponding calculation for a RRSP is more complicated. For the sake of argument, consider an individual who does not start saving for his retirement until age 30, but at that age is entitled to make the maximum annual contribution of $4000 to a RRSP[7] (i.e., his earned income must be at least $20,000 per year). He then contributes $4000 per year until he reaches age 65. The maximum pension he can acquire depends on the interest rate at which his savings accumulate and the interest rate used, given his expected mortality, to calculate the life annuity that he can buy at age 65 with his accumulated savings. The higher is the interest rate assumption used in both calculations, the higher will be the corresponding pension. If the retiree has a life expectancy of 15 years at age 65 (an unweighted average of the life expectancies of males and females at this age), the maximum pension is $26,342 if the interest rate is 4 per cent; $45,895 if the interest rate is 6 per cent; and $80,526, if the interest rate is 8 per cent. These results are, of course, only suggestive. They do indicate that given the current restrictions on both the maximum pension payable under a private pension plan and the maximum annual contribution to a RRSP, there is no reason to presume that the maximum pension payable under a RRSP is any less generous than the maximum pension payable under a private pension plan. In the illustration, a current market (nominal) return of about six per cent serves to equalize the maximum pension under the two schemes. If neither the maximum pension payable under a private pension plan nor the maximum annual

7 In the May 1976 budget this limit was raised to $5500. The maximum pension allowed a member of an employer pension plan was also increased.

contribution to a RRSP were indexed with respect to inflation, then an increase in the rate of inflation — which would ultimately be reflected in nominal market yields (see chapter three) — would increase the attractiveness of the RRSP relative to the private pension plan.[8]

PROPOSED LIBERALIZATION OF MINIMUM VESTING PROVISIONS: FURTHER ECONOMIC CONSIDERATIONS

On 27 September 1972, the Pension Commission of Ontario issued a 'Green Paper' concerning the vesting provisions contained in the Pension Benefits Act of Ontario. The 'Green Paper' proposed that the '45 and 10' rule be placed with a '40 and 5' rule; that is, pension benefits would be fully vested once an employee completed 5 years of service *and* reached age 40.

There are, of course, alternative ways in which the vesting provisions contained in the 1965 Act might be liberalized. The basic issues raised by liberalization may, however, be discussed in the context of this specific proposal. These issues relate to (1) income redistributive effects, (2) costs to the employer, and (3) the mobility of labour.

In contributory plans, the liberalization of the minimum vesting provisions under the Act is likely to have significant income redistributive effects among employees as well as between the employer and the employees, in the absence of compensating wage adjustments. An important input into the actuarial calculation of the level of contributions by both employer and employee necessary to fund the pension benefits provided by the plan is the employee turnover rate and hence the fraction of plan members in whom pension benefits are likely to vest. Employees who terminate employment without meeting the prescribed vesting requirements usually are entitled to both their accumulated contributions and interest on these contributions. The interest rate paid on these contributions is often below the rates obtainable in the marketplace, suggesting

---

8 Although the above comparison is useful, one should note that RRSPs differ in an important way from most employer pension plans. In particular, they do not have the scope to permit intergenerational transfers of income. Unit benefit plans, for example, can produce intergenerational transfers in at least three ways (Asimakopulos and Weldon, 1970): (1) benefits may be improved retroactively; (2) the assumptions under which the plans were costed could prove inaccurate and thus require transfers from firms' operating earnings; and (3) firms which operate partially funded plans (e.g., those which still have initial unfunded liabilities) may not have this future liability reflected in the market's evaluation of their net worth. The analogue to the RRSP would be the money purchase plan, in which pension benefits equal the accumulated amount of the total contributions made by or for the employee.

that the terminating employee suffers an income loss relative to the case where he had not joined the plan at all. In general, an effective liberalization of minimum vesting provisions would raise the contributions of both employees and the employer in order to sustain a *given level of plan benefits.* Income would thus be redistributed from the employer and employees whose benefits would have vested under the '45 and 10' rule to those employees whose benefits would not have vested under this rule. These latter employees too would pay higher contribution rates, but the effective increase in their income via the vesting of their pension benefits would clearly outweigh these higher contribution rates, since the latter would be dispersed equally between all employees and the employer.

In order to place the preceding discussion in perspective, one needs an estimate of the increase in the costs to (say) the employer of changing the minimum vesting requirements from the '45 and 10' rule to the '40 and 5' rule. Such estimates were prepared by the Ontario Pension Commission from data compiled by the Ontario Committee on Portable Pensions and were appended to its 1972 'Green Paper.' The estimates, as appended to the 'Green Paper,' are summarized in Tables 2 and 3. The estimates, based on a number of actuarial assumptions described in Appendix B to *Ontario Committee on Portable Pensions, Second Report* (Ontario, 1961), presume that the employer bears the entire burden of the increase in costs and that the new vesting provisions are not made retroactive. Estimates are presented for four representative types of plans (money purchase, unit benefit, final earning,[9] and flat benefit), for single and level premium funding, for contributory and non-contributory cases, for alternative turnover rates and for both males and females.

Note first that the cost of the proposed change in the vesting rule is considerably greater for money purchase plans than for unit benefit, final earnings, or flat benefit plans. This result reflects the fact, already noted, that the cost to the employer may be relatively small during the employee's younger years in a typical defined benefit plan. In a money purchase or defined contribution plan, on the other hand, the vested employee becomes entitled to the accumulated value of all past employer contributions on his behalf which will typically equal the accumulated value of the employee's own past contributions. Second, the cost to the employer is significantly higher in the non-contributory than in the contributory defined benefit plans. This result reflects the fact that the cost to the employer of benefits which vest in a

---

9 Final earnings plans are unit benefit plans in which the member's pension is based upon his length of service and his average earnings for a stated period just prior to his retirement.

TABLE 2

Impact on employer costs of liberalized vesting: single premium funding

Ratio of employer costs with vesting at age 40 and 5 years' service to that at age 45 and 10 years' service

Employee type	Money purchase (%)	Unit benefit plan (%)		Final earnings plan (%)		Flat benefit plan (%)	
		Contributory	Non-contributory	Contributory	Non-contributory	Contributory	Non-contributory
Males light turnover	105.2	101.4	103.4	100.7	103.1	102.0	103.2
Males medium turnover	105.7	101.7	103.7	100.7	103.6	102.4	103.6
Males heavy turnover	107.3	102.7	104.9	101.2	104.3	103.1	104.9
Females medium turnover	107.1	103.3	105.0	102.3	104.8	103.5	104.9
Females heavy turnover	109.0	104.0	106.2	102.9	106.1	104.8	106.2

SOURCE: Ontario (1972)
NOTES: Analysis assumes: (1) employers bear entire cost; (2) liberalized vesting has no impact on employee turnover; (3) vesting changes are not made retroactive

TABLE 3

Impact on employer costs of liberalized vesting: level premium funding

Ratio of employer costs with vesting at age 40 and 5 years' service to that at age 45 and 10 years' service

Employee type	Money purchase (%)	Unit benefit plan (%)		Final earnings plan (%)		Flat benefit plan (%)	
		Contributory	Non-contributory	Contributory	Non-contributory	Contributory	Non-contributory
Males light turnover	n/a	100.7	101.5	100.5	101.3	101.0	101.4
Males medium turnover	n/a	100.8	101.5	100.4	101.5	101.0	101.6
Males heavy turnover	n/a	100.8	101.7	100.2	101.6	101.1	101.8
Females medium turnover	n/a	101.2	102.0	100.8	101.8	101.3	101.9
Females heavy turnover	n/a	101.3	102.2	100.9	102.1	101.5	102.1

SOURCE: Ontario (1972)
NOTES: See Table 2

contributory plan is the difference between the actuarial value of the deferred pension and the accumulated value of the employee's contributions, while the cost in a non-contributory plan is the full actuarial value of the deferred pension to which the employee becomes entitled. As noted previously, the difference in the contributory plan is likely to be quite modest for a relatively young employee. Third, as is readily apparent, the costs to the employer are higher if the termination or turnover rate among his employees is high. Fourth, the costs to the employer are higher, the higher is the proportion of female employees. This result reflects the tendency for female employees on average to be younger than male employees, combined with the tendency for termination or turnover rates to be higher for young than for old employees. Finally, the increase in employer costs is significantly higher for all types of plans if single premium funding is employed. This result reflects the tendency, *ceteris paribus*, for the cost to the employer to rise more steeply with the age of the employee in the case of single premium relative to level premium funding.

To place the cost estimates contained in Tables 2 and 3 in further perspective, consider the costs to the employer in a contributory unit benefit plan which is funded by the level premium method. For male employees with a medium turnover rate, his costs would increase by 1.2 per cent. For contributory plans, which cover almost 80 per cent of all plans on a national basis (Canada, 1972a), the costs to the employer appear to increase only modestly, especially for the case of level premium funding. The money purchase plans, for which the increase in the cost to the employers is greatest, represented only 4.9 per cent of total plan members on a national basis in 1970, and this percentage continues to decline. In short, the figures cited in Table 2 combined with the actual distribution of plans by type and by contributory/non-contributory classification would tentatively suggest that the over-all increase in the cost to employers of moving to the '40 and 5' rule is not excessive and therefore should not serve as a major deterrent to the continued growth of private pension plans. Finally, all of the cost calculations presume that the employer bears the entire cost of the improvement in the vesting provisions. In fact, employers are likely to shift at least a portion of these costs to the employees in the form of higher contribution rates and/or lower wages.

The third economic consequence of a liberalization of statutory vesting provisions worthy of note is the possible impact on the mobility of labour. One may be tempted to conclude that the result would be to increase the mobility of labour. To the extent that effective wage grids are redesigned to enable firms to discourage labour turnover and to retain skilled employees, this conclusion would have to be qualified. In fact, evidence from the United States (US Congress, 1973) indicates that delayed vesting provisions may not have had a major deterrent impact on labour mobility in any event. The explanation for this tentative conclusion is in terms of the importance of emotional factors which may lead employees to leave jobs, combined either with a high rate of discount or possible ignorance of the value of the pension benefits so forfeited.

Of importance also is the possible deterrent impact of the proposed '40 and 5' rule on employer willingness to hire (in particular) older employees. At a given wage rate for any specified job, employers would have a stronger incentive to hire younger rather than older workers since the actuarial cost of hiring the latter will be higher in view of the increased likelihood that their benefits would vest. The tendency of employers, *ceteris paribus,* to prefer to hire younger than older workers is *not* discriminatory in an economic sense since the preference reflects an underlying difference in costs to the employer. At the same time, however, one should note that if the employer has the flexibility to pay the older worker a lower wage than the younger worker to reflect the *increase* in the actuarial pension cost of hiring the older worker, the deterrent to the hiring of the older worker could theoretically disappear. If one were to take age 65 as the normal retirement age, the potential disincentive for employers to hire older workers, *ceteris paribus,* should be most pronounced for workers aged 56 to 60. Such workers could simply not qualify for vesting under the current '45 and 10' rule, but clearly could do so under the '40 and 5' rule. Concern in the United States (US Congress, 1973) that liberalized vesting regulations may have made it more difficult for older employees to find jobs implicitly suggests that the flexibility of firms to compensate for the higher pension costs of older employers by offering them lower wages might be limited. If so, an additional impetus to the redesign of defined benefit plans to make them more age neutral (i.e., that the employer's share of pension costs does not increase with the age of the employee) is apparent.

SUMMARY

The recognition that pension benefits represent a form of deferred wages invites the recommendation – if one abstracts from administrative costs – that vesting be made full and immediate. Two important qualifications are important, however, and are frequently ignored in the discussion of this issue. First, a change to immediate vesting is likely to be accompanied by a change in effective wage grids as employers seek to provide greater rewards for longer service in order to retain skilled employees and to reduce turnover. The result would be to impose a cost on terminating employees which is similar in kind, although less discontinuous, than the cost imposed by delayed vesting. Second, earlier or immediate vesting might prove to be largely illusory in any event for members of contributory defined benefit plans, whose own contributions may purchase most of the benefits to which they become entitled during their younger years. Finally, the economic rationale for the 'locking-in' of both employee and employer contributions lies in the possible claim to income-tested, public retirement schemes if the worker fails to adequately save for his own retirement. The current regulations, however, may serve to penalize the member of an employer-sponsored private pension plan relative to the individual who saves for his own retirement in the form of a RRSP. This result will occur if the current wages of a worker who is a member of an employer-sponsored plan, *ceteris paribus,* are lower by an amount equal to the value of the employer's contribution than the current wages of a comparable worker who is not a member of such a plan. As noted previously, the recent study by Schiller and Weiss (1977) suggests that this will be the case, as does the general view that pension benefits — as a form of deferred wages — are part of the total compensation package with which employers compete for workers in competitive labour markets. The member of the employer-sponsored plan suffers by virtue of the fact that contributions made on his behalf are 'locked-in,' while those of the individual who saves in the form of an RRSP are not.

3

The impact of inflation:
the pre-retirement years

The erosion of pension funds by inflation, and hence of the pensions themselves,
is probably the least satisfactory thing about pension plans today.
Ontario Committee on Portable Pensions, *Second Report,* 1961

INTRODUCTION

For analytical purposes, the provision and preservation of an employee's pension
benefits in an inflationary climate can be treated in two stages: (1) the
preservation of the real value of pension benefits as they accumulate during the
employee's work years and (2) the preservation of the real value of these
benefits during his retirement years. Final earnings plans (and renegotiated flat
benefit plans) are the most successful of the popular pension plans in ensuring
the adequacy of pension benefits as they accumulate during the employee's
work years. In effect, inflation risk is borne by the employer rather than the
employee. Similarly the full indexation of pension benefits during the
employee's retirement years is required if the real value of the pension benefits
are not to be eroded by inflation which occurs after the employee has begun to
draw his pension. Full indexation exists currently for the CPP, the OAS, and for a
few private pension plans, most notably the superannuation plan for federal civil
servants.

The central issue addressed in this chapter is whether or not a final earnings
plan can remain actuarially sound in periods of high or accelerating inflation. In
institutional terms, the question is whether the actuarial deficiencies of final
earnings plans (in particular) which have materialized during the recent past are

unique to this inflationary period, or are likely to re-occur under similar circumstances. The central issue raised in the next chapter is whether private pension plans, in general, can provide fully indexed pension benefits during the employees' retirement years and yet remain actuarially sound. The resolution of both issues hinges on a common theme: the extent to which the real returns on the assets which comprise the investment portfolios of private pension plans are or are not neutral with respect to expected and unexpected inflation.

This chapter begins with a brief review of the major types of private pension plans and the extent to which each of them exposes the plan member to inflation risk. The sharp increase in the actuarial deficiencies of private pension plans which has accompanied the recent escalation in the rate of inflation in Canada is then reviewed. The increase in actuarial deficiencies is traced to the adverse impact of inflation on the real returns of both fixed-income securities and common stocks. This important result is followed by an analysis of the income redistributive effects of inflation on members (employees) and guarantors (employers) of private pension plans. An analysis of related institutional issues, including the amortization period for actuarial deficiencies and the eligible set of investment opportunities, completes the chapter.

ALTERNATIVE PENSION PLANS AND INFLATION RISK

As noted previously, there are three major types of private pension plans: unit benefit plans, flat benefit plans, and money purchase plans. Unit benefit plans, in turn, consist either of *career average plans,* under which the plan member accumulates each year a unit of pension equal to a percentage of his earnings in that year, and *final earnings plans* (including final average earnings and average best earnings plans), under which the member's pension is based upon his length of service and his average earnings (and usually average best earnings) for a stated period just prior to his retirement. The relative importance of these alternative pension plans, based both on the number of plans in operation and the number of plan members, is illustrated in Table 4 for the years 1960, 1965, and 1970.

The alternative plans as described above vary considerably in the extent to which the plan member is exposed to inflation risk, or the extent to which the pension benefits that accrue on his behalf may be eroded by inflation during his working years. Since wages and salaries in the aggregate rise at the same rate of inflation (plus real productivity gains), final earnings plans effectively ensure that a member's benefits will not be eroded by inflation which occurs during his employment years. A member of a career average plan, on the other hand, is likely to see the real purchasing power of his pension benefits eroded by inflation even as those benefits are accruing. Flat benefit plans, in which (for

TABLE 4

Plans and members by type of benefit, 1960, 1965, and 1970

	1960				1965				1970			
	Plans		Members		Plans		Members		Plans		Members	
	No.	%	No.	%	No.	%	No.	%	No.	%	No.	%
Unit benefit:												
Final earnings	28	0.3	10,793	0.6	44	0.3	23,434	1.0	16	0.1	5,613	0.2
Final average earnings	270	3.0	283,720	15.2	288	2.1	261,800	11.1	377	2.3	169,798	6.0
Average best earnings	117	1.3	632,295	34.0	238	1.7	859,771	36.7	970	6.0	1,260,917	44.7
Career average	2370	26.6	468,247	25.1	3956	29.0	667,224	28.5	4753	29.5	679,631	24.1
Level percentage of earnings	–	–	–	–	84	0.6	1034	–	46	0.3	2721	0.1
Totals	2785	31.2	1,395,055	74.9	4610	33.7	1,813,263	77.3	6162	38.2	2,118,680	75.1
Money purchase	5392	60.4	242,127	13.0	7758	56.8	152,738	6.5	8471	52.5	137,680	4.9
Profit sharing	211	2.4	23,616	1.3	351	2.6	28,253	1.2	310	1.9	21,374	0.8
Flat benefit	411	4.6	177,059	9.5	689	5.0	327,932	14.0	742	4.6	424,623	15.0
Composite	121	1.4	24,824	1.3	227	1.7	23,185	1.0	265	1.6	26,221	0.9
Other	–	–	–	–	25	0.2	277	–	187	1.2	93,758	3.3
Grand totals	8920	100.0	1,862,681	100.0	13,660	100.0	2,345,648	100.0	16,137	100.0	2,822,336	100.0

SOURCE: Canada (1970, 17)

example) a member receives a pension of x dollars per month for each year of service with a minimum service requirement of y years, also would appear to expose their members to inflation risk. In fact, however, flat benefit plans typically occur when the pension plans result from labour negotiations, and the level of benefits usually is increased during an inflationary environment as an integral part of subsequent collective bargaining negotiations. Finally, a member of a money purchase plan is also quite vulnerable to inflation risk, since his pension benefit is defined in terms of whatever amount contributions made on his behalf with interest will provide or purchase. Since contributions to a money purchase plan are usually expressed as a percentage of the employee's salary (with both the employer and the employee usually contributing on the latter's behalf), the result is to place greater weight on the employee's earnings early in life rather than later in life in determining his pension benefit since interest is earned for a much longer period of time on contributions made when the employee is young.

ACTUARIAL SOUNDNESS: THE PROBLEM OF EXPERIENCE
DEFICIENCIES

Under the Pension Benefits Act, employer liabilities with regard to private pension plans are divided into three categories: (1) *current service costs,* which must be fully funded on a yearly basis; (2) *initial unfunded liabilities* arising from the establishment of a new plan or an amendment of an existing plan, which must be amortized over a fifteen-year period; and (3) *experience deficiencies* which refer to any deficit determined at the time of review of a plan due to factors other than (i) any initial unfunded liability or (ii) the failure of an employer to make any payment as required by the terms of the plan, the Pension Benefits Act, or the regulations. Experience deficiencies arise, in effect, when the actuarial valuation of a pension plan indicates that the assumptions on which the employer's contributions were based were not borne out. They may thus arise from such factors as an unduly high longevity record for pensioners in situations where the fund assumes the mortality risk, an unexpected decline in earnings on the fund's investments, and unexpected increases in salaries and wages of employees. The Pension Benefits Act requires that experience deficiencies be amortized over a five year period.

During the recent period of accelerating inflation in Canada, bond prices have declined and the stock market has generally performed poorly. Thus one would predict that all trusteed pension plans are likely to be characterized by experience deficiencies which reflect, in essence, the poor performance of their investment portfolios. The sharp escalation in wages and salaries which has also

TABLE 5

Surplus or unfunded liability ($) per member, by type of plan

Plan type	Surplus	Initial unfunded liability	Experience deficiency	Unfunded liability
Career average	781	1444	29	1473
Final average	1333	2031	133	2164
Flat benefit	379	3737	23	3760
Composite	507	1326	32	1358
All types	749	2700	55	2755

SOURCE: Ontario (1975b, 6)

occurred in this period poses special problems for final earnings plans, whose benefits are effectively tied to wage and salary increases. One would predict that the recent period of accelerating inflation in Canada is likely to have produced dramatic increases in the experience deficiencies of final earnings plans.

Preliminary evidence in support of this contention is found in a recent study prepared by the Pension Commission of Ontario (Ontario, 1975b). The study is based on actuarial reports of the first 943 trusteed plans (out of a total universe of 2564 uninsured pension plans) filed during the 1971-3 period. Of particular interest is the information which is reproduced in Table 5. These figures indicate that the largest experience deficiencies were found in final earnings plans, although the magnitude of these deficiencies is still small relative to initial unfunded liabilities. One must note, however, that the reports from which these data were drawn were filed between 1971 and 1973, while the sharpest increase in inflation (to the two-digit level) did not occur in Canada until 1974. In short, the magnitude of the experience deficiencies of final earnings plans is likely to have increased greatly since the data for this study were filed. The various briefs submitted to the first public conference of the Canadian Association of Pension Supervisory Authorities (June 1975) provide qualitative support for this contention, as does J. Wells Bentley, the Superintendent of Pensions.

The central issue in terms of the actuarial soundness of final earnings plans is whether the large experience deficiencies which have occurred in the recent period of escalating inflation are attributable to unique features of this period, or whether they are likely to occur in any period of constant or accelerating inflation. The sharp escalation in the experience deficiencies of final earnings plans can be related, in essence, to the fact that their liabilities are effectively indexed with regard to inflation while the assets which comprise their portfolios are not. From this perspective, the issue of whether or not the experience deficiencies which have occurred in the recent period of escalating inflation are unique or predictable (and hence, likely to recur under similar circumstances) revolves on the neutrality with respect to inflation of the real returns on the assets – chiefly bonds and common stocks – which comprise private pension plans' portfolios (Table 6).

To examine this issue, one must first distinguish between expected and unexpected inflation. Expected inflation, as the term implies, refers to inflation which occurs but which had been predicted by market participants generally. Unexpected inflation represents the difference between realized inflation and expected inflation, and may be either positive or negative. The very rapid escalation in the realized rate of inflation in the past few years suggests, for example, that much of this inflation was probably unexpected.

The distinction between expected inflation is central to the conventional economic wisdom regarding the impact of inflation on the nominal – and hence on the real – returns on bonds and common stocks. Following Irving Fisher (1930), economists have long argued that the nominal interest rate on bonds will rise by the exact amount of any increase in the expected inflation rate during the maturity of the bonds. A rise in the expected inflation rate over (say) the next five years of one per cent, *ceteris paribus,* through the activities of both lenders and borrowers, will cause the nominal yield on bonds with a maturity of five years to rise by one per cent as well. The expected real return on bonds, equal to the nominal return less the expected rate of inflation, will thus be unchanged. An increase in the rate of inflation that was unexpected, however, would not have been incorporated into nominal interest rates and the realized real return on these bonds would fall accordingly. Similarly, economists have adhered to the viewpoint that the *real* return on common stocks would be unaffected by expected inflation, while the *real* return on the shares of an individual firm would rise (fall) if the firm were a net debtor (creditor) in response to unexpected inflation.[1]

These standard propositions, however, have been the subject of a considerable re-thinking in recent years. Tax considerations, for example, suggest that for the real after-tax returns to investors to be unaffected by expected inflation, nominal interest rates would have to increase by more than the (appropriately matched by maturity) rise in the expected rate of inflation (see: Darby, 1975; Carr, Pesando, and Smith, 1976). Further, to the extent that a higher and more volatile inflation rate creates greater uncertainty regarding the future course of nominal interest rates, risk-averting behaviour on the part of lenders may require

1 See Lintner (1975) and references contained therein.

TABLE 6

Asset distribution of trusted pension funds in the public and private sectors (book value), 1960, 1965-73

	Bonds		Stocks		Mortgages		Real estate lease-backs and miscellaneous		Pooled funds[1]		Mutual funds		Total	
	$'000,000	%	$'000,000	%	$'000,000	%	$'000,000	%	$'000,000	%	$'000,000	%	$'000,000	%
Public sector[2]														
1960	1174	83.7	16	1.1	130	9.3	50	3.6	3	0.2	29	2.1	1402	100.0
1965	1971	78.3	143	5.7	255	10.1	108	4.3	17	0.7	22	0.9	2516	100.0
1966	2187	76.9	189	6.7	293	10.3	130	4.6	21	0.7	24	0.8	2844	100.0
1967	2384	74.5	254	7.9	323	10.1	182	5.7	31	1.0	26	0.8	3200	100.0
1968	2618	73.3	344	9.6	352	9.8	194	5.4	38	1.1	28	0.8	3574	100.0
1969	2871	71.0	442	10.9	387	9.6	251	6.2	60	1.5	31	0.8	4042	100.0
1970	3258	69.5	510	10.9	509	10.9	299	6.4	77	1.6	33	0.7	4686	100.0
1971	3629	68.0	641	12.0	575	10.8	358	6.7	102	1.9	31	0.6	5336	100.0
1972	4118	67.5	841	13.8	627	10.3	370	6.1	119	1.9	28	0.4	6103	100.0
1973	4731	66.4	991	13.9	717	10.0	545	7.6	119	1.7	27	0.4	7130	100.0
Private sector[3]														
1960	1583	72.6	242	11.1	169	7.8	88	4.0	99	4.5	–	–	2181	100.0
1965	2211	54.9	846	21.0	368	9.1	179	4.5	411	10.2	10	0.3	4025	100.0
1966	2300	52.2	1028	23.3	383	8.7	191	4.3	492	11.2	12	0.3	4406	100.0
1967	2377	48.8	1260	25.9	401	8.2	237	4.9	579	11.9	14	0.3	4868	100.0
1968	2396	44.4	1610	29.8	424	7.9	309	5.7	642	11.9	17	0.3	5398	100.0
1969	2414	40.5	1983	33.3	476	8.0	378	6.3	689	11.6	21	0.3	5961	100.0
1970	2508	39.4	2170	34.1	513	8.0	440	6.9	720	11.3	22	0.3	6373	100.0
1971	2757	38.7	2573	36.1	595	8.4	388	5.4	792	11.1	20	0.3	7125	100.0
1972	2865	36.0	3060	38.5	669	8.4	468	5.9	858ʳ	10.8ʳ	27ʳ	0.4ʳ	7947	100.0
1973	2973	32.9	3430	37.9	834	9.2	692	7.7	1090	12.1	22	0.2	9041	100.0

TABLE 6 continued

	Bonds		Stocks		Mortgages		Real estate lease-backs and miscellaneous		Pooled funds[1]		Mutual funds		Total	
	$'000,000	%	$'000,000	%	$'000,000	%	$'000,000	%	$'000,000	%	$'000,000	%	$'000,000	%
Both sectors														
1960	2757	77.0	258	7.2	299	8.3	138	3.8	102	2.9	29	0.8	3583	100.0
1965	4182	63.9	989	15.1	623	9.5	287	4.4	428	6.6	32	0.5	6541	100.0
1966	4487	61.9	1217	16.8	676	9.3	321	4.4	513	7.1	36	0.5	7250	100.0
1967	4761	59.0	1514	18.7	724	9.0	419	5.2	610	7.6	40	0.5	8068	100.0
1968	5014	55.9	1954	21.8	776	8.6	503	5.6	680	7.6	45	0.5	8972	100.0
1969	5285	52.8	2425	24.3	863	8.6	629	6.3	749	7.5	52	0.5	10,003	100.0
1970	5766	52.2	2680	24.3	1022	9.2	739	6.6	797	7.2	55	0.5	11,059	100.0
1971	6386	51.2	3214	25.8	1170	9.4	746	6.0	894	7.2	51	0.4	12,461	100.0
1972	6983	49.7	3901	27.8	1296	9.2	838	6.0	977ʳ	6.9ʳ	55ʳ	0.4ʳ	14,050	100.0
1973	7704	47.6	4421	27.4	1551	9.6	1237	7.6	1209	7.5	49	0.3	16,171	100.0

1 Includes segregated funds.
2 Includes the following types of organizations: municipalities and municipal enterprises, provincial crown corporations and government agencies, federal crown corporations and government agencies, and educational institutions and organizations.
3 Includes the following types of organizations: regions and charitable, health, trade and employee associations, cooperatives, incorporated and unincorporated businesses and others.

SOURCE: Canada (1973, 19, Table D)

a premium to be built into nominal yields to compensate for this uncertainty. Finally, in perhaps the most important reconsideration, the two standard propositions regarding the impact of both expected and unexpected inflation on the rate of return on common stocks are undergoing intensive investigation (see: Lintner, 1975; Nelson, 1976).

In order to provide some Canadian evidence on the extent to which the real returns on bonds and common stocks were neutral with respect to both expected and unexpected inflation, econometric analysis of these issues was conducted, and the results are reported in considerable detail in Appendix A. In brief, the conclusions from this study are as follows: (1) nominal interest rates do appear to adjust in such a fashion as to match changes in the expected rate of inflation; (2) nominal interest rates do *not* appear to incorporate a premium to compensate lenders for the risks associated with increased uncertainty about the future course of inflation and hence increased uncertainty about the future course of nominal interest rates; and (3) the real return on common stocks, at least for holding periods of four years or less, varies *inversely* with both expected and unexpected inflation.

The conclusions regarding the impact of inflation on the real returns on common stocks appear to conflict with the conventional wisdom and hence merit further comment (see Pesando, 1977). First, these results mirror those obtained by other investigators who have employed United States data, including Branch (1974), Body (1976), Lintner (1975), and Nelson (1976). Second, these results are *not* unique to the postwar period, the sample period employed in the econometric work reported in Appendix A. Lintner, for example, concludes that the real returns associated with holding common stocks fall in response to an increase in inflation on the basis of his study using annual (United States) data for the full 1900-71 period. Third, the conclusion that an increase in inflation *per se* is associated with a reduction in the real return of common stocks is easily reconciled with the fact that, over long periods of time, the average rate of return on common stocks has tended to exceed the average rate of inflation. The latter result is traditionally invoked by those who argue that equities represent an adequate *long-term* hedge against inflation. In fact, this result conveys no information whatsoever regarding the impact of inflation *per se* on equity returns, but only that the multiplicity of factors which determine the rate of return on common stocks have interacted in such a fashion so as to produce a long-term, positive real return (i.e., an average market return in excess of the average rate of inflation). By decomposing the 1900-66 period into sub-periods corresponding to high inflation, low inflation, and stable prices, for example, Sydney Homer obtained results (Litner, 1973) which suggested that the higher the inflation rate, *ceteris paribus,* the lower the real return on common stocks. His results, in addition, are consistent with those obtained by Pesando (1977, 32-37).

The evidence cited above is especially important in light of the fact that the Pension Benefits Act of 1965 permits up to 100 per cent of the funds of non-insured plans or insured plans using the segregated fund principle to be invested in common stocks. The Act, in effect, invites private pension plans to avail themselves of the presumed tendency of the market yield on equities to exceed the rate of inflation, at least over long periods of time. In passing, one should note that data compiled by Statistics Canada (Canada 1973c) indicate a steady increase (Table 6) during the past 15 years in the importance of common stocks in pension plan investment portfolios. In 1973, for example, equities represented 37.9 per cent of the assets of pension plans in the private sector, and 13.9 per cent for pension plans in the public sector.

The analysis above has centered on the distinction between expected and unexpected inflation and their impact on the real returns available on both bonds and equities. Of crucial importance, in addition, is the further distinction between *anticipated* and *unanticipated* inflation. Expected inflation can be anticipated only if economic agents can adjust their behaviour in such a way as to ensure that the inflationary environment leaves their real wealth or real income unaffected. The fact that nominal interest rates appear to adjust on a one-for-one basis with changes in the expected inflation rate, for example, is not sufficient to ensure that the real return on an investment portfolio consisting entirely of bonds will be unaffected by the change in the expected rate of inflation. This fact reflects the presence of bonds acquired at various points in time, and whose nominal terms are thereby fixed for various periods into the future, in the portfolios of most private pension plans. An increase in the expected rate of inflation, by raising all nominal interest by a corresponding amount, reduces the market value of the existing bonds in the portfolio and thus lowers its real return. Note, by way of contrast, *if* the real return on equities were unaffected by expected inflation, then a portfolio consisting entirely of common stocks would enable the pension plan to anticipate the expected inflation. The absence of vintage effects in an equity portfolio also suggest that if the real return on equities were unaffected by both expected and unexpected inflation, then a portfolio consisting entirely of common stocks would enable the pension plan to anticipate all inflation, whether expected or unexpected.

To sum up, portfolios consisting (1) entirely of bonds, (2) entirely of equities, or (3) some combinations of the two are *not* capable of anticipating inflation, even if that inflation is expected. Experience deficiencies of final earnings plans are thus likely to increase in a period of accelerating inflation and to decrease in a period of decelerating inflation.

THE INCOME REDISTRIBUTIVE EFFECTS OF INFLATION IN THE CONTEXT OF PRIVATE PENSION PLANS

The economic costs of unexpected inflation relate to its effects on the distribution of income. This fact raises the question of the income redistributive effects of inflation in the context of private pension plans. In particular, does inflation produce a real wealth transfer from plan members (employees) to guarantors (employers) and, if so, does this transfer occur both prior to and after retirement? The answer to this question not only provides a useful perspective on the issues raised earlier in this chapter, but also has potential implications for future regulation in this area.

Consider a typical defined benefit plan in which the plan member is promised a minimum pension based on his number of years of service and a selected period of earnings. A plan member, for example, might draw a pension of a per cent of the average salary of the highest, normally the last, n working years for each of his b years of service. The accumulated contributions of both the employer and the plan member are used to purchase a life annuity for the member at the time of his retirement. To the extent that these accumulated funds are not sufficient to purchase the annuity, the employer contributes the difference. Algebraically, the amount of the member's pension benefit (B) is related to his salary (S_i) in his last n work years as follows:

$$B = ab \; (\sum_{i=1}^{n} S_i)/n. \tag{1}$$

The present value (P) of an annuity which provides the indicated benefits can be expressed in terms of the interest rate employed in actuarial calculations (r) and the member's life expectancy in years (x) as follows:

$$P = \sum_{i=0}^{x} B/(1+r)^i \; . \tag{2}$$

The first point to note is that the plan member will suffer a real wealth loss *during his pre-retirement years* in the form of a decline in the real value of his defined benefits in the presence of realized inflation, regardless of whether the inflation is expected or unexpected. On the assumption that the real pre-retirement earnings of the plan member are unaffected by inflation, the plan member *will* suffer a real wealth loss because his benefits are defined in terms of his *average* earnings during the last n years prior to his retirement. In an inflationary climate, the defined benefit formula involves the summation of dollars with different purchasing power. Compared to the case of zero inflation, the real value of the member's pension will be unaffected by inflation only if n is equal to one. Indeed, this result underlies the recent growth of final earnings plans (n small) at the expense of career average plans (n large) in response to the need to preserve the real value of a plan member's pension benefits as they accumulate during his work years.

For this real wealth loss of the employee to be reflected in a corresponding gain to the employer, however, requires that the real rates of return on the plan's assets be unaffected by realized inflation. Since fixed-income securities and common stocks constitute the vast majority of assets of private pension plans, this result requires that the real returns on these two assets be unaffected by inflation, regardless of whether that inflation is expected or unexpected. The results cited earlier in this chapter indicate that an increase in either expected or unexpected inflation *ceteris paribus* depresses the real return on a portfolio consisting of fixed-income securities and/or common stocks. In short, one cannot presume that the real wealth loss of the employee is mirrored by a corresponding real gain to the employer, although this would be the case if the real returns to the plan's assets were neutral with respect to inflation. When inflation occurs, the real change in the liabilities of the pension plan *ceteris paribus* will fall owing to the averaging process cited earlier. At the same time, however, the real return to the pension plan's assets *ceteris paribus* will fall if the tentative conclusions cited earlier are valid. The guarantor will be a net beneficiary in any inflationary period only if the former effect exceeds the latter. In general, one must conclude that the net impact of inflation on the real wealth of the employer is ambiguous, although the plan member unambiguously suffers a real wealth loss.

The second point is that the plan member will also suffer a real wealth loss when inflation occurs during his *post-retirement years,* regardless of whether the inflation is expected or unexpected. This loss reflects the fact that, according to the defined benefit formula, the employee's pension is fixed in nominal dollars. Once again, however, one cannot determine whether the employer is a net beneficiary of this real wealth loss. Consider the case of *expected* inflation. If nominal returns – and ultimately the interest rates used in actuarial calculations – rise in response to expected inflation, the amount of capital necessary to purchase a given, fixed-dollar annuity will fall (Deutsch, 1975). In the context of equation (2), once B is determined, the present value (P) of the annuity will fall if the interest rate used in the actuarial calculations mirrors the increase in expected inflation. Since the guarantor must purchase the annuity, the temptation is to conclude that he benefits from expected inflation. If the real returns on the plan's assets *were* unaffected by expected inflation, and if the interest rate assumptions employed in actuarial assumptions did increase (as do interest rates in the market place) in response to an increase in expected inflation, then the presumed transfer of wealth to the guarantor would take place. Once again, however, one must note the earlier evidence which suggests that the real return on the plan's assets is likely to fall in an environment of realized inflation, regardless of whether the inflation was expected or unexpected.

In summary, the member of a defined benefit plan does suffer a real wealth loss in the presence of realized (expected plus unexpected) inflation during his work years, unless the plan is of the final earnings variety. The plan member also suffers a real wealth loss from inflation which occurs during his retirement years. One cannot, however, unambiguously conclude that the guarantor is a net beneficiary of this wealth transfer. To the extent that the guarantor is *not* a net beneficiary, the combined loss in real income of the member and guarantor, *ceteris paribus,* must be reflected in an increase in the real income of other economic agents. The issuers of fixed income securities are the most obvious beneficiaries of such an income transfer.

RELATED POLICY ISSUES

The preceding analysis provides a useful framework in which to examine a number of policy issues regarding the regulation of private pension plans. Three such issues, the amortization period for experience deficiencies, the funding of private pension plans in an inflationary climate, and the eligible set of investment opportunities, are analyzed in turn.

The amortization period for experience deficiencies
The central theme of this chapter has been that final earnings plans are the most successful of the alternative private pension plans in ensuring the adequacy of pension benefits as they accumulate during the employee's work years. In turn, this result suggests that the Government of Ontario ought to give consideration to changes in the Pension Benefits Act and/or its regulation, in order to promote their growth.

The most obvious way in which the province may make progress toward this goal is to liberalize the amortization period for experience deficiencies. Final earnings plan are likely to be characterized by sharp increases in experience deficiencies during periods of escalating inflation. The five-year amortization period prescribed by law thus imposes an onerous burden on plan managers, especially in view of the fifteen-year amortization period alloted initial unfunded liabilities. Thus a flat benefit plan whose benefits are revised in response to an inflationary climate is granted fifteen years to amortize the resulting initial unfunded liabilities, as would a career average plan whose benefits are liberalized for a similar reason. Ignoring the distortion to the incentives to adopt final earnings as opposed to career average plans (with subsequent ad hoc adjustments to deal with inflation), the question of whether experience deficiencies ought to be treated differently from initial unfunded liabilities merits investigation in its own right.

First and foremost, one should note that the existence of experience deficiencies and/or initial unfunded liabilities does not imply that if a plan were wound up it would not be able to meet all of its earned pensions. In general, and as emphasized by the Canadian Institute of Actuaries (1975), the triennial valuations serve two distinct purposes. The first is to indicate the solvency position of the plan if it should be terminated on the valuation date. If the value of the assets is less than the value of the liabilities on a termination basis, then the authorities may wish to require the rapid amortization of any such unfunded amount. Note that such a policy would be indifferent as to whether the deficit were called an experience deficiency or an initial unfunded liability. Such termination liabilities might consist of the liabilities incurred for pensioners, for terminated vested employees, for ongoing vested employees, for other beneficiaries, for non-vested ongoing employees with respect to their own contributions plus accrued interest, for all required employee contributions and accrued interest not reflected in these earlier categories, and for all voluntary employee contributions plus accrued interest.

The second purpose of the valuation reports is the determination of the plan's contributions on an ongoing basis. Actuarial deficiencies calculated on this basis, whether termed experience deficiencies or initial unfunded liabilities, could be amortized over much longer periods.

The above scheme is only meant to be suggestive. Considerable debate, for example, would arise concerning the determination of termination liabilities for the solvency test, such as whether all accrued liabilities − not just vested benefits plus employee contributions − should be included in the calculation of termination liabilities as defined above. The major point, however, is twofold: first, experience deficiencies and/or initial unfunded liabilities *per se* are not evidence of a plan's insolvency; and second, the logic for the more stringent requirements for experience deficiencies compared to initial unfunded liabilities appears hard to understand. As a result, firms are not only discouraged from creating final earnings plans, but also firms with such plans are discouraged from strengthening their actuarial assumptions.

In the *Employee Retirement Income Security Act of 1974* (US Congress, 1974), the United States formally adopted a plan termination scheme designed to insure participants and beneficiaries against loss of benefits arising from a complete or partial termination of the private pension plan. Any recommendation to extend amortization period for experience deficiences, or for both experience deficiencies and initial unfunded liabilities, invites the question of whether or not such a liberalization must be accompanied by a termination insurance scheme. Indeed, this issue received considerable attention in the First Annual Conference of the Canadian Association of Pension Supervisory Authorities (June 1975).

The argument in favour of termination insurance requires considerable qualification in the Canadian context. First, the private pension plans of most small firms – the ones that are the most likely to face the prospect of forced termination – consist of individual or group annuities. Indeed, two-thirds of all Canadian pension plans are underwritten through group annuity contracts with insurance companies, although they represent only one-quarter of the membership and one-fifth of the assets. Under these group annuity contracts, the insurance company accepts funds from the employer and promises to pay certain units of pension in return for the money received. Participants in these plans, in effect, already possess plan termination insurance.

Second, as noted previously, one cannot infer from published data on experience deficiencies and/or initial unfunded liabilities the need for or magnitude of plan termination insurance. This viewpoint is emphasized by the Pension Commission of Ontario (Ontario, 1975) and reflects the distinction between solvency versus ongoing valuation procedures discussed previously. (Any deficit on a solvency or termination basis would presumably constitute the base against which the insurance premiums would be levied.)

In general, the principle of termination insurance is an important one if employee benefits are to be fully protected. In view of (1) the lack of evidence to indicate the urgent need for the adoption of such a scheme in Canada,[2] (2) the complexity of designing and administering such a scheme, and (3) the more stringent funding requirements in Canada, the postponement of the decision

---

2 J. Wells Bentley, Superintendent of Pensions, indicates in private conversation that the loss of benefits to employees upon the winding up of plans in Ontario simply has not proved (at least to date) to be a major problem. Indeed, effective 15 November 1973 the Pension Benefits Act was amended with the primary objective of strengthening the rights of employees in the event that the employer goes bankrupt or in the case of mergers or acquisitions. In the event of termination of a plan, the Act requires provision to be made for payments to all employees covered under the plan up to the date of the winding up of the plan. Before assets of the plan can be distributed, a report must be filed with the Pension Commission of Ontario and no assets can be distributed without the permission of the commission.

regarding the adoption of termination insurance would appear to be in order. The greatest advantage of such a postponement might well be the opportunity to monitor the United States experience in this area, which may well prove to be the efficient strategy if the Canadian evidence later supports the adoption of termination insurance.

The funding of private pension plans in an inflationary climate
Until recently, tax regulations also served to discourage the growth of final earnings plans. Section 20 of the Department of National Revenue's 'Information Circular No. 72-13R2 Employees' Pension Plans, explicitly precluded incorporating into salary projections an allowance for the possible effects of inflation.[3] This rule, in effect, was in direct conflict with the thrust of the Pension Benefits Act which requires plans to make adequate funding provisions. To a large extent, this provision virtually guaranteed that final earnings plans (especially) would be characterized by sharp increases in experience deficiencies during periods of accelerating inflation, thereby exacerbating the problems noted earlier in this chapter. This anomaly serves to highlight the contradictory regulations which govern the funding of private pension plans. On the one hand, the Department of National Revenue has developed an extensive set of rules for acceptable plan provisions and financing and administrative arrangements, and the major impact of these rules is to limit the tax-sheltered benefits provided to pension plans to reasonable amounts. The Pension Benefits Act of Ontario, by establishing minimum funding requirements for private pension plans, may occasionally be in conflict with the Department of National Revenue's goal of preventing unreasonable or excessive, tax-sheltered contributions to such plans.

The Department of National Revenue's 'Information Circular No. 72-13R3 – Employees' Pension Plans,' dated 1 December 1975, reduced the tax disincentive to the growth of final earnings plans. Paragraph 22(a) of the revised circular provides: 'In cases of plans which provide for pension benefits based on best or final average earnings at retirement, these benefits may be funded on the basis of anticipated increase in salaries which reflect promotional, productivity and economic increases provided that the long-term assumption adopted for the salary scale is reasonably consistent with the long-term assumption concerning the rate of return on assets; normally the latter should exceed the former by at

---

3 Section 22, paragraph (1), reads: 'A projection of remuneration to normal retirement age, if warranted on the basis of remuneration paid in prior years, is acceptable in principle for the purpose of determining the obligation to the employee under the fund or plan. *The projection should not have regard to the effect of possible inflation*' (italics added).

least 1 percentage point.' This revision in the tax environment is significant for two reasons: first, it permits the incorporation of inflation forecasts into wage projections; and second, it disciplines the size of tax-deductible contributions by invoking a relationship between nominal interest rates and the rate of inflation. The latter point merits additional comment.

The empirical results cited in this chapter suggest, *ceteris paribus,* that a one per cent increase in the expected rate of inflation will raise nominal or market interest rates by one per cent as well. Nominal interest rates can thus be decomposed into an *ex ante* real interest rate plus the *expected* rate of inflation. In equilibrium, when inflationary expectations are realized, nominal interest rates can be decomposed into a real interest rate plus the *observed* rate of inflation. Similarly, the constancy over long periods of time in the relative income shares of capital and labour (Branson, 1972) suggest that wage increases consist, in equilibrium, of the sum of the real rate of growth of productivity plus the rate of inflation. From this perspective, the statutory requirement implies that the implicit real interest rate employed in actuarial calculations exceed the rate of growth of productivity by one per cent. If one accepts the two per cent productivity figure employed by the Anti-inflation Board, a real interest rate of three per cent is the minimum rate that must be employed if a productivity figure consistent with historical data is used in the wage projections. Data on realized returns to holders of different categories of debt (Government of Canada bonds, corporate bonds, etc.) are not readily available in Canada. Evidence from the United States (Ibbotson and Sinquefield, 1975) suggests that this three per cent figure is high relative to the historical (real) returns to both government and corporate bonds, but less than the long-term (real) return to common stocks.

One should also note that the revised statute is *not* likely to eliminate the tendency for a rise in the actual rate of inflation to be accompanied by an increase in the experience deficiencies of final earnings plans. Inflationary expectations appear to adjust with reasonably long lags to changes in actual rates of inflation, so that a rise in the actual rate of inflation will only gradually produce an increase in market rates of interest. To the extent that the wages respond more quickly to changes in the actual rate of inflation, an increase in the rate of inflation is still likely to produce an increase in experience deficiencies, and conversely. This result, in turn, would appear to strengthen the earlier argument for an extension of the amortization period for experience deficiencies.

The eligible set of investment opportunities
In general, the preceding arguments suggest, *ceteris paribus,* the desirability of broadening the eligible set of investments to which private pension plans can commit their funds in order to help insulate the real returns to their asset

portfolios from fluctuations in the rate of inflation. In essence, the liabilities of final earnings plans are indexed with respect to inflation, while their assets are not. The ideal asset would be an index bond or its equivalent. The issue of the possible provision of index bonds by the public and/or private sectors is extremely complex and receives attention in the following chapter. The more immediate – and less ambitious question – is the extent to which the problems faced by final earnings plans in an inflationary climate could be mitigated by broadening the scope of their investment options.

The 'basket clause' (Section 14 of the Regulations to the Act) permits funds to invest up to a maximum of seven per cent of the book value of the total assets of the fund in investments such as real estate. This flexibility to invest in real estate, however, is reduced by the provision that the investment in any one parcel of real estate cannot exceed two per cent of the book value of the total assets of the fund. The logic of introducing the possibility of investing in real estate, of course, reflects the need for private pension plans to acquire assets whose real values will not be eroded by inflation. If a subsequent study were to indicate that real estate holdings, especially if adequately diversified, were an effective inflation hedge, then one might be able to make a persuasive case for liberalizing the flexibility of the investment options accorded private pension plans in this area. In this regard, one should note further that the lack of liquidity of real estate holdings should probably not be used as an argument to dissuade their inclusion in pension plan portfolios since pension benefits are paid out over a prolonged period of time and other sources of income from the asset portfolio and/or employee-employer contributions should be able to smooth out discontinuities arising from the sale of real estate holdings.

In general, the flexibility to extend the set of eligible investments so as to reduce the sensitivity of the real return of a pension plan's portfolio to fluctuations in the rate of inflation is limited. A liberalization of restrictions on real estate investments may be of some value, but the ideal represented by an index bond will remain very difficult to approximate in practice.

SUMMARY AND CONCLUSIONS

This chapter began with the observation that of the popular private pension plans, those of the final earnings variety represent the most effective means of ensuring that the real value of pension benefits as they accumulate during an employee's work years will not be eroded by inflation. The text then turned to an analysis of the key problems posed by the current inflationary climate for final earnings plans. This analysis identified the sharp increases in experience deficiencies of these plans as the most important problem and noted that final earnings plans could remain actuarially sound in an inflationary climate only if the real returns on their assets holdings were neutral with respect to both expected and unexpected inflation.

The problem of rising experience deficiencies in an inflationary climate was traced to the fact that the liabilities of final earnings plans are effectively indexed with respect to inflation, while their assets are not. An empirical study of the impact of inflation on the rates of return on bonds and equities, summarized in Appendix A, tentatively suggests that the real return on portfolios consisting of bonds and/or equities are likely to fall in periods of accelerating inflation. In short, the assets which comprise the portfolios of most private pension plans are not likely to permit them to anticipate inflation. Experience deficiencies thus are predicted to increase in periods of accelerating inflation, regardless of whether the inflation is expected or unexpected, and conversely.

An analysis of income redistributive effects of inflation indicate that, for a typical defined benefit plan, the employee suffers a real wealth loss in both his pre-retirement and his post-retirement years. In general, the question of whether or not the employer would be a net beneficiary of this wealth transfer is ambiguous. If private pension plans, including those of the final earnings variety, could invest their funds in index bonds, then they could remain actuarially sound in an inflationary climate (i.e., they would not suffer an increase in experience deficiencies) *and* they could also provide for fully indexed pension benefits after retirement and yet continue to remain actuarially sound. The income redistributive effects of inflation, in the context of private pension plans, would disappear.

The central theme of this chapter has been that final earnings plans are the most successful of the alternative private pension plans in ensuring the adequacy of pension benefits as they accumulate during the employee's work years. In turn, this result suggests that the Government of Ontario ought to give consideration to changes in the Pension Benefits Act and/or its regulation to promote their growth. Central in any list of recommended changes to this effect is the liberalization of the amortization period for experience deficiencies.[4]

4 Shortly after this chapter was written, the Ontario Pension Benefits Act Regulations were amended (December 1976) to permit a substantial proportion of experience deficiencies to be amortized over a fifteen-year period. In brief, an actuary may now determine an experience deficiency by performing a 'test' valuation in addition to the regular valuation. If the experience deficiency is less under the 'test' valuation, which may use less conservative assumptions, than under the regular valuation, the difference is treated as an initial unfunded liability and can be amortized over a fifteen-year period. The deficiency under the 'test' valuation must still be amortized over five years. In general, this change in the regulations is very much in the spirit of the changes recommended in the text, and helps to remove one obstacle to the growth of final earnings plans.

4
The impact of inflation:
the post-retirement years

From time to time proposals have also been made for the issue of government and possibly other securities of guaranteed purchasing power, known as index bonds, as an alternative to common shares. If a measure of this type were found practicable the vulnerability of pension funds to inflation might be overcome.
Ontario Committee on Portable Pensions, *Second Report,* 1961

INTRODUCTION

The sharp escalation in the rate of inflation in Canada in recent years has served to focus attention anew on the issue of whether or not private pension plans can provide indexed pension benefits during an employee's retirement years. Indeed, one can argue persuasively that if the private pension system cannot respond to this need,[1] then private pension plans must — and ultimately will — be absorbed into larger government programs, as recommended by the Canadian Labour

---

1 In a recent book, Calvert (1977) argues that private pension plans should, at most, be only partially indexed for inflation. He bases his argument on his analysis of data pertaining to income and expenditure patterns of the aged, from which he concludes that cash needs decline with age. Unfortunately, his conclusions cannot be drawn from the data he examines. The apparent decline in certain consumption expenditures of the aged in his sample simply reflects, in all probability, the decline in incomes of the aged. Further, if one were willing to accept the argument that the real incomes of the aged should be allowed to fall, there is no reason to let the decline be determined arbitrarily by the rate of inflation.

TABLE 7

The erosion of a fixed-dollar pension in an inflationary climate

Inflation Rate	Age	Value of pension in real dollars (as per cent of initial value[1])					
		65	70	75	80	85	90
0%		100	100	100	100	100	100
2%		100	91	82	74	67	61
4%		100	82	68	56	46	38
6%		100	75	56	42	31	23
8%		100	68	46	31	21	15
10%		100	62	39	24	15	9
12%		100	57	32	18	10	6

1 For example, if the rate of inflation is 4 per cent, then the real value of the fixed-dollar pension, ten years after the pensioner's retirement at age 65, will equal 68 per cent of its initial value.

Congress. The extent to which inflation during an employee's retirement years erodes the real purchasing power of a fixed-dollar pension is illustrated in Table 7. If, for example, inflation proceeds at six per cent per year, then the real value of a fixed-dollar pension ten years after the employee's retirement will have fallen to 56 per cent of its initial value. One can place this issue in further perspective by noting, for example, that the University of Toronto's Institute for Policy Analysis (1975) is currently projecting an average rate of inflation of close to five per cent for the period 1976-85.

For all intents and purposes, private pension plans today do not provide for the full indexation of pension benefits during the employee's retirement years.[2] Many employers have responded to the needs of retired employees in the current inflationary climate by ad hoc adjustments to pensions which are currently in force. In 1974, for example, International Nickel voluntarily increased pensions for retired employees, although the increases were not sufficient to match the rise in the cost of living. These ad hoc adjustments, however, appear to be severely inadequate in light of the facts that both the CPP and OAS are fully indexed with respect to inflation, and that the Supplementary Retirement

2 Some firms, such as Shell Canada, apparently are trying to devise schemes to enable them to provide fully-indexed pension benefits (Richard Gwyn, 'Private pension plans simply out-of-date,' Toronto Star, 14 June 1975, C1).

Benefits Act (which received royal assent on 14 September 1973) provides for the full indexation of pensions for retired federal civil servants.

The question of whether or not private pension plans are capable of providing fully indexed pension benefits is a multi-faceted one. Under the current institutional setting, for example, tax regulations play an important role. Until recently, the Department of National Revenue did not allow any pension contribution to be deductible from taxable income if it was in payment for increases in benefits anticipated as a result of inflation. Until recently, and in direct conflict with the Federal tax regulation, provinces required that any allowance for inflation be fully funded in advance. As a result, employers could not write indexed pensions into their plans and were effectively compelled to rely on ad hoc adjustments. Effective 3 September 1975, however, Ontario amended the Pension Benefits Act to permit companies to commit themselves to cost of living adjustments for retired employees and to pay for these adjustments on a pay-as-you-go basis. In December, 1975, the Department of National Revenue revised its regulations to grant tax deductibility status to payments made in anticipation of cost-of-living adjustments to the pensions of retired employees. The Information Circular, dated 1 December 1975, contains the following provision (paragraph 23) regarding supplementary pension benefits after retirement:

In cases of plans which provide for adjustments to pensions in payment after retirement in recognition of increases in the cost of living ..., these benefits may be funded on the basis of anticipated long-term increases in the Consumer Price Index in future years, in regard to both retired and active employees, provided that the long-term assumption adopted for the anticipated increases in the Consumer Price Index in future years is reasonably consistent with the long-term assumption concerning the rate of return on assets. Normally the latter should exceed the former by at least 2 per centage points.

(Note that the relationship between the assumptions regarding the *nominal* rate of return on assets and the rate of inflation, which serves to discipline the magnitude of the permitted deductions, is consistent with a *real* rate of return on assets of two per cent per year. Note also that this requirement is *less* stringent – assuming real productivity increases of two per cent a year – than the requirement (see chapter three) that the interest rate assumption exceed the wage growth assumption by one per cent.)

In short, recent changes in the tax and regulatory environment reflect the growing awareness of the limitations of fixed-dollar pensions in any inflationary climate, together with the desire (at least) not to discourage private pension plans from committing themselves to cost-of-living adjustments to pensions in force. Certain limitations still exist, however. The provincial regulation provides the pension plan with the option of prefunding the cost-of-living adjustment or funding it on a pay-as-you-go basis. If the cost-of-living adjustments are not fully funded (i.e., if they are only partially funded or funded on a pay-as-you-go basis), the retired employee's pension would likely have to be reduced back to the unindexed level if the plan were wound up. The amendment (to Regulation 654) provides:

Where a pension plan is terminated or wound up in whole or in part, any escalated adjustment (cost of living adjustment) ... to which a member or a former member affected by the termination or winding up is entitled, whether such escalated adjustment is currently being paid or has not yet commenced, shall, to the extent that it has not been prefunded, not adversely affect any pension or other benefit which would otherwise have been provided under the plan when it is terminated or wound up.

In short, private pension plans now find themselves in a tax and regulatory environment which is much more favourable to their providing for the indexation of pension benefits after the employee's retirement. The key issue, however, rests on the question of whether or not a fully-funded private pension plan can provide for the indexation of pension benefits and yet remain actuarially sound. Significantly, the CPP, OAS, and Public Service Superannuation Plan are all funded, at least in part, on a pay-as-you-go basis. Alternatively, all draw upon the taxing powers of the government to ensure that any deficits in the corresponding funds do not present an obstacle to the provision of the promised pension benefits. Many observers conclude that no fully-funded private pension plan can remain actuarially sound and provide for fully indexed pension benefits. Robert M. MacIntosh (1976), executive vice-president of the Bank of Canada, succinctly summarizes the popular view: ' ... it is impossible in practice for private pension funds to do what the public sector pension fund now does. That is to say, it is impossible to fund for future benefits fully escalated to the cost of living index by earning a rate of return or assuming a rate of return sufficient to pay for those benefits.' In a similar vein, the Toronto *Globe and Mail* contrasts the Public Service Superannuation Plan with those opportunities afforded a private pension plan: 'Private pension plans have no public treasury behind them to cover gaps. They have to stand on their own, by law be actuarially sound, and, as they now work, the option of indexing is virtually denied. How can an actuarily sound pension plan be fully indexed when inflation is an unruly variable that cannot be calculated in advance? ('Bonanza for the Mandarins,' *The Globe and Mail*, 5 December 1975)

These representative viewpoints would appear to suggest that private pension plans cannot remain actuarially sound and yet provide fully indexed pension benefits. In fact, closer analysis of this issue indicates that private pension plans *could* provide fully indexed pension benefits and remain actuarially sound if the real returns on the assets which comprise their portfolios were unaffected by inflation. If the real returns on these assets were neutral with respect to both expected and unexpected inflation, then private pension plans could remain actuarially sound regardless of the actual rate of inflation. Those commentators who argue that private pension plans cannot remain actuarially sound and provide fully indexed benefits are *implicitly* arguing that available investment vehicles do not possess this neutrality property.

The fact that a private pension plan could provide fully indexed benefits if the real returns to its portfolio were unaffected by inflation is illustrated in the next section of this chapter. The previous evidence regarding the impact of inflation on the real returns on common stocks and fixed-income securities is briefly re-evaluated in the context of this proposition. The fourth section of the chapter contains an analysis of some of the issues relevant to the provision of index bonds, the classic investment vehicle whose real return is unaffected by inflation. An overview of alternative ways in which the indexation of benefits after retirement may be approximated and/or achieved completes the chapter.

ACTUARIAL SOUNDNESS OF FULLY-INDEXED PENSION BENEFITS AND THE NEUTRALITY OF REAL RETURNS

A formal proof of the proposition that a fully-funded pension plan can remain actuarially sound and provide fully indexed pensions for retired employees if the real returns on the fund's assets are also fully indexed with respect to inflation is contained in a brief appendix to this chapter. The proposition is perhaps better understood with the aid of the numerical example summarized in Table 8.

Consider a pension plan which provides a fixed-dollar pension in a non-inflationary climate. In the example depicted in Table 8, a plan is presumed to provide a pension of $0.25 per quarter ($1.00 per year) for the duration of the pensioner's life. For purposes of illustration, the pensioner at the time of his retirement is assumed to have a life expectancy of 80 quarters (20 years). The table indicates that at an assumed interest rate of one per cent per quarter (approximately 4.06 per cent per year) an initial capital sum of $13.72 (approximately) is sufficient to provide the indicated pension.[3] In other words,

3 To provide a pension of $2.00 per year, *ceteris paribus,* would require an initial capital sum of $27.44 (2 times $13.72), and so on.

TABLE 8

Indexed pension benefits and the neutrality of real returns:
an example of actuarial soundness

CASE I: *No inflation, no indexation of pension benefits.* Pension = $1
per year ($0.25 per quarter); interest rate = one per cent per quarter;
initial capital to purchase 20-year (80-quarter) annuity = $13.72204.
START = capital at beginning of quarter; EARN = earnings on the
capital during the quarter; PAY = pension benefit paid in quarter;
LEFT = capital at end of quarter.

	START	EARN	PAY	LEFT
1	13.722040	0.137221	0.250000	13.609270
2	13.609270	0.136093	0.250000	13.495360
3	13.495360	0.134954	0.250000	13.380310
4	13.380310	0.133803	0.250000	13.264110
5	13.264110	0.132641	0.250000	13.146750
6	13.146750	0.131468	0.250000	13.028220
7	13.028220	0.130282	0.250000	12.908500
8	12.908500	0.129085	0.250000	12.787590
9	12.787590	0.127876	0.250000	12.665460
10	12.665460	0.126655	0.250000	12.542120
11	12.542120	0.125421	0.250000	12.417540
12	12.417540	0.124175	0.250000	12.291710
13	12.291710	0.122917	0.250000	12.164630
14	12.164630	0.121646	0.250000	12.036280
15	12.036280	0.120363	0.250000	11.906640
16	11.906640	0.119066	0.250000	11.775700
17	11.775700	0.117757	0.250000	11.643460
18	11.643460	0.116435	0.250000	11.509900
19	11.509900	0.115099	0.250000	11.374990
20	11.374990	0.113750	0.250000	11.238740
21	11.238740	0.112387	0.250000	11.101130
22	11.101130	0.111011	0.250000	10.962140
23	10.962140	0.109621	0.250000	10.821760
24	10.821760	0.108218	0.250000	10.679980
25	10.679980	0.106800	0.250000	10. 536780
26	10.536780	0.105368	0.250000	10.392150
27	10.392150	0.103921	0.250000	10.246070
28	10.246070	0.102461	0.250000	10.098530
29	10.098530	0.100985	0.250000	9.949516
30	9.949516	0.099495	0.250000	9.799011
31	9.799011	0.097990	0.250000	9.647001
32	9.647001	0.096470	0.250000	9.493471
33	9.493471	0.094935	0.250000	9.338406
34	9.338406	0.093384	0.250000	9.181789
35	9.181789	0.091818	0.250000	9.023607
36	9.023607	0.090236	0.250000	8.863843

TABLE 8, *Case I*, continued

	START	EARN	PAY	LEFT
37	8.863843	0.088638	0.250000	8.702481
38	8.702481	0.087025	0.250000	8.539506
39	8.539506	0.085395	0.250000	8.374901
40	8.374901	0.083749	0.250000	8.208650
41	8.208650	0.082087	0.250000	8.040735
42	8.040735	0.080407	0.250000	7.871142
43	7.871142	0.078711	0.250000	7.699853
44	7.699853	0.076999	0.250000	7.526851
45	7.526851	0.075269	0.250000	7.352118
46	7.352118	0.073521	0.250000	7.175639
47	7.175639	0.071756	0.250000	6.997396
48	6.997396	0.069974	0.250000	6.817369
49	6.817369	0.068174	0.250000	6.635543
50	6.635543	0.066355	0.250000	6.451898
51	6.451898	0.064519	0.250000	6.266417
52	6.266417	0.062664	0.250000	6.079081
53	6.079081	0.060791	0.250000	5.889871
54	5.889871	0.058899	0.250000	5.698769
55	5.698769	0.056988	0.250000	5.505755
56	5.505755	0.055058	0.250000	5.310813
57	5.310813	0.053108	0.250000	5.113920
58	5.113920	0.051139	0.250000	4.915059
59	4.915059	0.049151	0.250000	4.714210
60	4.714210	0.047142	0.250000	4.511352
61	4.511352	0.045114	0.250000	4.306464
62	4.306464	0.043065	0.250000	4.099528
63	4.099528	0.040995	0.250000	3.890523
64	3.890523	0.038905	0.250000	3.679428
65	3.679428	0.036794	0.250000	3.466222
66	3.466222	0.034662	0.250000	3.250883
67	3.250883	0.032509	0.250000	3.033391
68	3.033391	0.030334	0.250000	2.813725
69	2.813725	0.028137	0.250000	2.591862
70	2.591862	0.025919	0.250000	2.367780
71	2.367780	0.023678	0.250000	2.141457
72	2.141457	0.021415	0.250000	1.912870
73	1.912870	0.019129	0.250000	1.681998
74	1.681998	0.016820	0.250000	1.448818
75	1.448818	0.014488	0.250000	1.213305
76	1.213305	0.012133	0.250000	0.975438
77	0.975438	0.009754	0.250000	0.735193
78	0.735193	0.007352	0.250000	0.492545
79	0.492545	0.004925	0.250000	0.247470
80	0.247470	0.002475	0.250000	−0.000055

TABLE 8

CASE II: *Inflation, indexation of pension benefits.* Pension = $1 per
year ($0.25 per quarter) but is fully indexed[1]; inflation rate = 2.4 per
cent per quarter; interest rate (real) = one per cent per quarter; yield
on portfolio = 1 per cent (real) plus 2.4 per cent (inflation adjustment)
or 3.4 per cent per quarter; initial capital to purchase 20-year
(80-quarter) annuity *still* = $13,722.04.

	START	EARN	PAY	LEFT
1	13.722040	0.466550	0.256000	13.932590
2	13.932590	0.473708	0.262143	14.144160
3	14.144160	0.480902	0.268435	14.356620
4	14.356620	0.488125	0.274877	14.569870
5	14.569870	0.495376	0.281474	14.783770
6	14.783770	0.502648	0.288229	14.998190
7	14.998190	0.509939	0.295146	15.212980
8	15.212980	0.517242	0.302229	15.427990
9	15.427990	0.524552	0.309483	15.643060
10	15.643060	0.531864	0.316910	15.858010
11	15.858010	0.539173	0.324516	16.072660
12	16.072660	0.546471	0.332304	16.286810
13	16.286810	0.553752	0.340279	16.500280
14	16.500280	0.561010	0.348445	16.712840
15	16.712840	0.568237	0.356808	16.924250
16	16.924250	0.575425	0.365371	17.134300
17	17.134300	0.582566	0.374139	17.342720
18	17.342720	0.589653	0.383118	17.549250
19	17.549250	0.596675	0.392313	17.753600
20	17.753600	0.603622	0.401728	17.955490
21	17.955490	0.610487	0.411369	18.154580
22	18.154580	0.617256	0.421242	18.350580
23	18.350580	0.623920	0.431351	18.543150
24	18.543150	0.630467	0.441704	18.731900
25	18.731900	0.636885	0.452304	18.916450
26	18.916450	0.643160	0.463159	19.096450
27	19.096450	0.649279	0.474274	19.271450
28	19.271450	0.655229	0.485657	19.441020
29	19.441020	0.660995	0.497312	19.604690
30	19.604690	0.666559	0.509247	19.761990
31	19.761990	0.671908	0.521469	19.912420
32	19.912420	0.677023	0.533983	20.055450
33	20.055450	0.681885	0.546799	20.190530
34	20.190530	0.686478	0.559922	20.317090
35	20.317090	0.690781	0.573359	20.434500
36	20.434500	0.694773	0.587119	20.542140
37	20.542140	0.698433	0.601210	20.639350
38	20.639350	0.701738	0.615638	20.725440

TABLE 8, *Case II,* continued

	START	EARN	PAY	LEFT
39	20.725440	0.704665	0.630413	20.799680
40	20.799680	0.707189	0.645543	20.861310
41	20.861310	0.709285	0.661035	20.909540
42	20.909540	0.710925	0.676899	20.943550
43	20.943550	0.712081	0.693144	20.962470
44	20.962470	0.712724	0.709779	20.965400
45	20.965400	0.712824	0.726814	20.951400
46	20.951400	0.712348	0.744256	20.919470
47	20.919470	0.711262	0.762118	20.868600
48	20.868600	0.709533	0.780408	20.797710
49	20.797710	0.707122	0.799137	20.705670
50	20.705670	0.703993	0.818316	20.591320
51	20.591320	0.700105	0.837955	20.453460
52	20.453460	0.695418	0.858065	20.290780
53	20.290780	0.689887	0.878658	20.102000
54	20.102000	0.683468	0.899745	19.885710
55	19.885710	0.676114	0.921339	19.640470
56	19.640470	0.667776	9.943450	19.364790
57	19.364790	0.658403	0.966092	19.057090
58	19.057090	0.647941	0.989277	18.715740
59	18.715740	0.636335	1.013019	18.339030
60	18.339030	0.623527	1.037331	17.925210
61	17.925210	0.609457	1.062225	17.472440
62	17.472440	0.594063	1.087718	16.978770
63	16.978770	0.577278	1.113823	16.442230
64	16.442230	0.559036	1.140553	15.860710
65	15.860710	0.539264	1.167926	15.232040
66	15.232040	0.517890	1.195955	14.553980
67	14.553980	0.494835	1.224657	13.824160
68	13.824160	0.470021	1.254048	13.040130
69	13.040130	0.443365	1.284144	12.199350
70	12.199350	0.414778	1.314962	11.299160
71	11.299160	0.384172	1.346521	10.336810
72	10.336810	0.351452	1.378837	9.309435
73	9.309435	0.316521	1.411927	8.214028
74	8.214028	0.279277	1.445812	7.047493
75	7.047493	0.239615	1.480511	5.806597
76	5.806597	0.197424	1.516042	4.487979
77	4.487979	0.152591	1.552426	3.088143
78	3.088143	0.104997	1.589683	1.603457
79	1.603457	0.054518	1.627834	0.030141
80	0.030141	0.001025	1.666901	−1.635735

1 Pension in quarter t = ($0.25) (1 + inflation rate per quarter)^t

the interest income and gradual amortization of an initial capital sum of $13.72 will provide an annual pension of $1.00 per year, paid in quarterly instalments, for 20 years if the rate of interest is one per cent per quarter, or slightly more than four per cent per year. At the end of the 80 quarters (20 years), the initial capital has been entirely exhausted. The time path through which the initial capital is depleted is portrayed in the table.

In the context of this example, the issue of whether or not a fully-funded private pension plan can remain actuarially sound and provide for fully-indexed benefits for retired employees can be restated as follows. Is an initial capital sum of $13.72, which may be regarded as the current dollar value of the accumulated contributions on behalf of the employee at the time of his retirement, sufficient to purchase a *real* pension of $1.00 per year in an inflationary climate on the assumption that the real interest rate remains at one per cent per quarter? The example in the second part of Table 8 illustrates the answer to this question. The rate of inflation during the employee's retirement years is assumed in the illustration to be constant at 2.4 per cent per quarter (approximately 10 per cent per year).[4] The nominal return on the plan's portfolio would thus be 3.4 per cent per quarter; that is, equal to the one per cent real interest rate plus the compensation for the 2.4 per cent quarterly rate of inflation. The real value of the pension is to remain at $0.25 per quarter so that the current dollar value of the pension would grow at a compound rate of 2.4 per cent per quarter.

As Table 8 illustrates, the initial capital sum of $13.72 is sufficient, on the basis of the assumptions cited above, to provide a real or constant-dollar pension of $1.00 per year for 20 years in the highly inflationary climate embodied in the example. In other words, to provide a fully-indexed pension for the retired employee requires an unchanged initial sum of capital so long as the real return earned on the capital sum is also unchanged at one per cent per quarter; that is, so long as the real return on the plan's assets is unaffected by inflation. After 20 years (80 quarters), and ignoring rounding errors, the initial capital sum is finally exhausted. Note that the current-dollar value of the initial capital sum peaks (at a value of $20.97) 44 quarters after the employee has started to draw his pension. The real or constant-dollar value of the initial capital sum (not shown), however, declines steadily throughout the employee's retirement years just as in the earlier example pertaining to a non-inflationary climate. Note also that the current dollar value of the *quarterly* pension payment rises to $1.66 in the 80th quarter, more than six times its initial value.

---

4 The proposition holds in the case of a variable rate of inflation as well. Note the proof contained in the appendix to this chapter.

COMMON STOCKS AND FIXED-INCOME SECURITIES:
NEUTRALITY OF REAL RETURNS?

The most obvious example of an asset whose real return is independent of the
rate of inflation is an index bond, which simply promises its holder a predeter-
mined real return and adjusts its nominal return in such a fashion so as to ensure
that the holder receives the promised real return. Since index bonds do not exist
in Canada, the question of whether or not a fully-funded private pension plan
can provide for the full indexation of benefits after retirement centres on the
issue of the neutrality of the real returns on fixed-income securities and common
stocks – the major investment vehicles of private pension plans – with respect
to both expected and unexpected inflation. The evidence summarized in chapter
three indicated that an increase in either expected or unexpected inflation will
depress the real return on a portfolio consisting of fixed-income securities and/or
common stocks. This result suggests that a pension plan whose funds were invested primarily in these assets could not provide fully-indexed pensions and yet
remain actuarially sound in an inflationary climate.[5]

There do exist stylized conditions under which the negative impact of an
increase in the rate of inflation on the real return on both fixed-income
securities and common stocks would *not* prevent a pension fund which held
these assets from approximating the situation of neutrality with respect to both
expected and unexpected inflation. These conditions include: (1) an equal
(future) probability of increases and decreases in both expected and unexpected
inflation and (2) sufficiently rapid fluctuations between net increases and
decreases in expected and unexpected inflation so as to ensure that their *net*
impact on real returns will be zero for even short periods of time. The likelihood
of the first condition being satisfied is subject to debate, while the likelihood of
the second is practically nil. The result is that one must conclude that, for
practical purposes, there currently exists no financial instrument whose real
return can be reasonably presumed to be unaffected by either expected or
unexpected inflation. Since the regulatory provisions effectively require than
private pension plans concentrate their investment funds in financial assets, one

5 Note that if, for any future period, the probability of an increase in either expected or
  unexpected inflation equals the probability of a decrease in either expected or unexpected inflation, then over sufficiently long periods the net impact of future inflation
  on these real returns will be zero. This result underlies the assumption in the simulation
  experiments reported in subsequent chapters of this book that the real interest rate is
  constant and unaffected by the rate of inflation. For long periods such as the ones
  pertaining to the simulation of the distributional impact of the CPP, the assumption of
  a constant real return is satisfactory from both a theoretical and an empirical viewpoint.

must further conclude that private pension plans are not able in today's financial environment to provide fully-indexed pension benefits if they are to remain actuarially sound.

THE INDEX BOND: A PRACTICAL ALTERNATIVE?

The previous results have indicated that fully-funded private pension plans could provide indexed pension benefits, both pre- and post-retirement, if they could channel their investment funds into assets whose real returns were unaffected by both expected and unexpected inflation. *If* index bonds were widely available in the Canadian capital market, then private pension plans which invested their funds exclusively in these bonds could – in principle – provide fully-indexed pension benefits and remain actuarially sound. Since index bonds do not exist in Canada, the analysis in this chapter would not be complete without identifying the central issues and/or complications arising from the introduction by the private and/or public sectors of index bonds.

As a point of departure, one might ask the question *why* neither the government nor corporations have issued index bonds in Canada. The probable demand by investors for index bonds in today's inflationary climate would suggest, *ceteris paribus,* that borrowers could issue index bonds at a lower *ex ante* real interest rate than the rate at which they could issue conventional (nominal) bonds.[6] Turning first to the private sector, many commentators have argued that corporations are effectively precluded from issuing index bonds because of the open nature of the commitment to bondholders. This argument merits qualification, however, in view of the impact of inflation on the nominal returns to the capital investment which was financed by the issuance of index bonds. In many (if not most) instances, an increase in the rate of inflation will not only increase the current dollar costs of servicing the index bonds, but also the current dollar returns from the investment project. Many firms may thus find themselves capable of assuming the inflation risk inherent in the issuance of index bonds. The major impetus to private companies to issue index bonds may come, however, from the difficulty they are experiencing in raising long-term funds in today's highly inflationary – and uncertain – environment. In recent

6 For a more formal analysis of the relationship between the real return on index and nominal bonds, see Fischer (1975). He concludes that the real return required to induce an investor to hold an index bond will be below the expected real return on a nominal bond if the real return on common stocks is negatively correlated with the rate of inflation, and conversely. The evidence cited earlier in this text suggests that the real return on common stocks *is* negatively correlated with inflation.

years, the proportion of new corporate debt represented by long-term borrowing has dropped sharply as risk-averse lenders and borrowers seek to avoid long-term commitments which subject them to the risks associated with a rise or fall in the future rate of inflation (see Pesando, 1977, 27-9). This reduction in long-term financing, in turn, has greatly complicated the problem of corporate planning and induced at least one major Canadian corporation to seriously consider the option of issuing an index bond.[7]

The non-issuance of index bonds by the government also merits comment. Unlike corporations, the various levels of government possess taxing powers which would enable them to assume the open commitment implicit in the issuance of index bonds. The almost secular rise in inflation in the past decade, much of which was apparently unexpected, has undoubtedly served to reduce the interest cost to the government of financing its deficits in the conventional manner relative to the cost if it had issued index bonds. The relevance of this experience may, however, be quickly disappearing. At today's high interest rates, which reflect Canada's recent experience with inflation, the possibility that the government may incur higher costs by issuing traditional rather than index bonds is a real one. Unexpected declines in the rate of inflation, in short, may be equally likely as unexpected increases.

In analysing the policy option of the government's issuing index bonds or in assessing the likelihood that private corporations may elect to issue index bonds, one must emphasize the far-reaching consequences of such action. The issuance of index bonds by the government, for example, could lead via competitive forces to the introduction of indexed financial instruments such as savings deposits, mortgages, and corporate bonds in the private sector. Indexation might quickly percolate through the financial system and ultimately produce a Canadian capital market which is distinctly different from the one that exists today. The extent to which indexed instruments either complemented or replaced traditional financial arrangements would ultimately be determined by the extent of the demand for indexed instruments. The introduction of index bonds by the government would raise related issues such as changes in the tax treatment of interest income (see: Bossons, 1974; Pesando, 1977), and might raise the fear in certain circles that the government would lessen its commitment to price stability as a goal of economic policy (Giersch et al., 1974).

In general, the issue of index bonds is so complex — and the potential ramifications so great — that one can only note the importance of further

---

7 David M. Culver, President, Aluminum Company of Canada Limited has expressed in private conversations his interest in this option.

research in this area (see: Pesando, 1977, 72-8). Any recommendation as to whether the government ought to issue index bonds and/or encourage the private sector to do so, must await the outcome of such research. The fact that the availability of index bonds would enable the private pension system to fully index pension benefits and yet remain actuarially sound does, of course, strengthen the argument on their behalf. Further, the demand by investors for index bonds, which will *ultimately* determine whether or not they will be introduced, will undoubtedly increase if the inflation rate in Canada remains high and volatile.

THE INDEXATION OF PENSION BENEFITS DURING THE EMPLOYEE'S RETIREMENT YEARS: THE OPTIONS

One can argue persuasively that the private pension system can survive in Canada only if it can, in effect, provide indexed benefits to pensioners. Proposed pension reforms in the United Kingdom, Holland and Switzerland, for example, require that private pensions be indexed. In order to provide indexed benefits to pensioners and yet remain actuarially sound, private pension plans must be able to invest their funds in assets whose real returns are unaffected by inflation. Neither fixed-income securities nor common stocks, the principle assets held by private pension plans, possess this property. The classical investment vehicle which does provide the necessary hedge against inflation, the index bond, is not currently available in the Canadian capital market. If index bonds were to become available, private pension plans could provide for the full indexation of pension benefits. (Such a move would, however, entail a one-shot increase in unfunded liabilities if – as is likely – indexation were extended to past service benefits.) The introduction of index bonds in Canada would, as noted previously, raise a number of complex problems. These problems in turn raise doubts as to whether index bonds would ever be introduced.

In light of these circumstances, what can one say about the likely evolution of the private pension system in Canada? As noted previously, recent changes in federal tax laws combined with revisions in Ontario's Pension Benefits Act have made it easier for employers to commit themselves to adjustments to pensioners to compensate for inflation. Compared to the superannuation plan for federal civil servants as well as to the CPP and OAS, the private pension system still appears to be wanting in terms of cost-of-living protection to retired employees. Many pension specialists argue that in the absence of an indexed financial instrument, the responsibility of providing indexed pensions must ultimately fall on the government. A submission by the Life Underwriters Association of Canada (1975) to the Canadian Association of Pension Supervisory Authorities reflects, in one specific statement, the general concern: 'The concept of an employer having to face the open ended and uncontrollable cost of indexing pensions 20 or 30 years into the future for retired employees is frightening and is probably quite unrealistic for the vast majority of employers to consider. Either some arbitrary ceiling will have to be imposed or indexing or its cost beyond such ceiling, will ultimately have to become a charge on general tax revenues.'

If the absence of an index bond or equivalent effectively prevents private pension plans from committing themselves to the full indexation of pension benefits, the extent to which the real returns to their investments approximate the necessary inflationary hedge may facilitate (1) their committing themselves to more generous, partial compensation, and/or (2) more nearly adequate ad hoc adjustments. In this regard, one can raise the question of whether, over time, the real returns on private plan's portfolios are likely to become more insulated from inflation. Variable rate mortgages, short-term bonds, and real property, for example, are assets which might better approximate the inflation neutrality of index bonds. If private pension plans, regulations permitting, were to more fully avail themselves of these investment vehicles, the real performance of the portfolios might become less sensitive to inflation. Significantly, several trust companies in Canada have introduced, albeit on a modest scale, short-term mortgages. Short-term mortgages, in turn, represent a move toward variable rate mortgages, which are a step closer to the benchmark of an index bond. In short, the responsiveness of the financed system to the apparent demand for the elimination of inflation risk is apparent, although still rudimentary. The implications of this responsiveness for the longer-term ability to provide financial instruments whose real returns are less sensitive to inflation is encouraging, with corresponding implications for the ability of private pension plans to increase the protection to pensioners with regard to inflation. If so, one should be careful *not* to extrapolate too quickly the implications of recent experience in this regard.

As a final observation, one must comment on the popular view that life insurance companies cannot write annuities which are indexed with respect to inflation. At the time of the employee's retirement, there exists a pool of funds representing the current value of past contributions on his behalf which can be used to purchase an annuity. In theory, one might argue that the underwriter of an annuity could offer an indexed benefit, with the underwriter assuming the inflation risk in return for a lower expected pension for the retired employee. The fundamental problem with this suggestion is, of course, the fact that under-writers are *not* in a position to comfortably assume this inflation risk since they have no readily apparent way in which to hedge *their* positions. They, too, lack an investment vehicle whose real return is not likely to be influenced by infla-tion.[8] Alternatively, if life companies were to write indexed annuities, they would be under great pressure to reduce their vulnerability to inflation risk by acquiring indexed financial instruments. The result would be a greatly increased demand by life companies for index bonds or their equivalent. In turn, this would enhance the attractiveness to corporations of issuing index rather than traditional bonds by, *ceteris paribus,* lowering the required *ex ante* return on the index bonds. Corporations, which would be in the position of issuing index bonds to finance the purchase of real assets, would be clearly more capable of assuming the inflationary risk.

APPENDIX[9]

Proof of the actuarial soundness of an inflation-indexed pension fund
Consider an annuity of initial capital W_0 which draws a constant nominal interest rate r and pays at a constant nominal-dollar rate y. Then the capital of the annuity W follows:

$$dW/dt = rW - y. \tag{1}$$

Consider an inflation-indexed annuity of initial capital W_0' in which the capital W' draws interest at a rate $r + (dP/dt)/P$ and pays at a rate $p \cdot y$. Assume $p(0) = 1$, and P bounded, continuous, and non-zero. Then W' follows:

$$dW'/dt = [r + (dP/dt)/P]W' - py. \tag{2}$$

Let T be the time at which the annuity is exhausted, i.e., $W(T) = 0$. One wants to show that $W_0' = W_0$ implies $W'(T) = 0$; that is, the inflation indexed annuity is actuarially sound.
Let $Z = pW$. Then

$$dZ/dt = (dp/dt) W + (dW/dt)P = (dP/dt)W + prW - py =$$

$$[r + (dp/dt)/P] (pW) - py.$$

8 The fact that, historically, equities have provided a positive real return over the long haul (Cagan, 1974) does not provide a solution to the life company's problem. If infla-tion were to remain high or to accelerate, then *ceteris paribus* the real return to common stocks would be low or perhaps negative. Life companies which wrote indexed annuities would likely suffer losses, perhaps for a prolonged period of time, which would effec-tively preclude their moving in this direction.
9 This proof is due to Charles P. Cohen.

Hence, Z and W' obey the same first-order differential equation. Only one initial value is needed to fix W' and Z. Since $p(0) = 1$, $W_0 = W'$ implies $Z_0 = W_0'$ which implies $Z(t) = W'(t)$. Hence, $W(T) = 0$ implies $Z(T) = 0$ which implies $W'(T) = 0$.

Note that this proof, unlike the example contained in Table 2, does not require that the rate of inflation be constant.

PUBLIC PENSION PLANS

5
Canada's public programs for the aged

Canada has legislated many programs that provide retirement incomes. These programs are diverse in their approaches. Some are of the income maintenance variety, others are lump sum payments to those over 65, while others are contributory. In addition there are several significant tax advantages for those over 65. The various programs are described in this chapter. In subsequent chapters important issues affecting the design of the programs will be analysed and possible modifications will be considered.

THE CANADA PENSION PLAN

The Canada Pension Plan is a comprehensive program that not only provides for retirement income, but also for survivor, orphan and disability benefits, and benefits for the children of disabled contributors. At least superficially, the plan appears to be reasonable. It is for the most part indexed for inflation and does not attempt to combine income maintenance functions with what is supposed to be a contributory program. Income support for those without contributions is left to OAS, GIS, and provincial programs. The only obvious anomaly is an implicit subsidy to those with families. The extent of this subsidy will be indicated in chapter seven.

Contributions
The CPP benefits are financed out of contributions paid since 1966 by employers and employees. The contribution rate for both employer and employee is 1.8

per cent of annual earnings between the year's basic exemption ($700 in 1975) and the year's maximum pensionable earnings ($7400 in 1975). The self-employed pay both employer and employee contributions. The year's maximum pensionable earnings (YMPE) is scheduled to increase at a 12.5 per cent annual rate until it catches up with the average earnings as measured by the industrial composite of Statistics Canada. With a 5 per cent rate of inflation and a 2.5 per cent rate of growth in real wages, this will occur in 1981. Thereafter YMPE will increase at the same rate as average earnings. If current rates of inflation persist, the YMPE might never catch up to the industrial composite. The year's basic exemption is 10 per cent of the year's maximum pensionable earnings. Contributions are not paid by (1) those earning less than the basic exemption, (2) agricultural workers who earn less than $250 from each employer, (3) those in casual labour (e.g., babysitters), and (4) other special cases such as provincial government employees (unless an agreement has been reached between the province and the federal government). For practical purposes the plan is universal for those not covered by the Quebec Pension Plan.

Contributions are made between the ages of 18 and 70, or until retirement benefits are claimed. Most individuals will find it in their best interest to claim benefits at age 65 (see next section).

Retirement benefits
Retirement benefits are payable at age 65. They are based on the relationship between a worker's earnings and the year's maximum pensionable earnings. Simplifying somewhat, the ratio of earnings to the YMPE (the ratio is set equal to one if earnings exceed the YMPE) is averaged for each year after the worker turned 18 (or the year 1966). This time span is called the contribution period.[1] The resulting fraction (or the value one) is multiplied by the YMPE average for the year of retirement and the two previous years. The result is called the average pensionable earnings (AYMPE). The annual retirement pension is 25 per cent of the average pensionable earnings. Thereafter, the pension increases annually with the Consumer Price Index. To illustrate the calculation in the simplest case, assume that someone earned more than the YMPE in every year between ages 18 and 65. His pension would be 25 per cent of the average YMPE for the years in which he was 63, 64, and 65. At the end of 1975 the maximum pension was $1620.

When one has contributed for more than ten years, 15 per cent of the months in the contribution period may be dropped before computing the average

1 For those immigrating after age 18, the years from age 18 are included in the contribution period.

pensionable earnings.[2] This allows one to disregard the periods with the lowest earnings. Similarly, for each month worked after age 65 an additional month of low earnings may be dropped.[3] One therefore has a choice of whether or not to apply for benefits at age 65 or wait as long as five years. This provision appears to be relevant for only special cases. An additional year of work may increase real benefits, but it also increases contributions and results in the loss of one year's benefits. As an example, given a *real* rate of interest of 2½ per cent and current mortality rates, a dollar of added benefits per year from age 66 on is worth $10.35 at age 65 for men and $13.11 for women. This present value of additional benefits must be compared with the contributions paid and benefits foregone in the 65th year.[4] An additional reason for continuing to contribute would be to establish rights to spouse's benefits. The spouse's benefits require a minimum number of years of contributions, described below.

Death, spouse, and orphan benefits
Benefits other than for retirement require a minimum qualifying period. A person qualifies for death, spouse, and orphan benefits if he contributes for either (1) at least three calendar years and one-third of the number of calendar years in his contribution period, or (2) for at least ten calendar years. Benefits are in part based on the average pensionable earnings of the deceased whether or not he had reached retirement age. Lump sum death benefits equal one-half of the annual retirement pension (calculated at time of death if he or she was not receiving retirement benefits) or 10 per cent of the year's maximum pensionable earnings, whichever is the lesser.

Orphan benefits are payable to an unmarried child under 18 or an unmarried child under age 25 who is in school. Benefits in 1975 were $447.00 per year, to be increased in the future with the Consumer Price Index.

---

2 The reference to months is somewhat misleading. Subject to minor exceptions earnings are deemed to be received for each month of a year in which contributions are made.

3 Drop out months are allowed only if the resulting total exceeds 120.

4 It is worthwhile to contribute for an additional year (year t) if

$$(\text{Cont}_t + \text{Ret}_t^t) < \sum_{j=1}^{\infty} \left\{ \left[(\text{Ret}_{t+j}^{t+1} - \text{Ret}_{t+j}^t) S_{t+j}^t \right] / (1+i)^j \right\} ,$$

where Cont_t are the contributions for year t; Ret_{t+j}^t are the benefits claimed in year t and paid in year $t+j$; S_{t+j}^t is the probability of surviving from year t to year $t+j$; i is the nominal rate of interest.

Surviving spouse's benefits depend on age, presence of children, and whether or not the spouse is disabled. The surviving spouse under age 65 with children, or one who is disabled, receives a flat benefit ($447.00 in 1975) plus 37.5 per cent of the deceased contributor's retirement pension (calculated as if he or she retired). At age 65 the surviving spouse's benefits become 60 per cent of the deceased spouse's retirement benefit, adjusted for price changes. The surviving spouse who is (1) under 35 when the contributor dies, (2) has no children, and (3) is not disabled, receives no benefits until age 65. At that time benefits are payable if he or she is not married. Spouses between ages 35 and 45 when the contributor dies (or when the children cease to receive benefits) receive benefits proportionally reduced. At age 36, ten per cent of the full benefits are received, and so on up to age 45. Since 1975, benefits have been payable to widowers and to widows on the same basis.

Disability benefits
A contributor who is under age 65 and who is found to be suffering from a severe and prolonged disability is eligible to receive benefits if he has contributed for at least five calendar years.[5] The disability pension is a flat amount ($447.00 in 1975) plus 75 per cent of the contributor's retirement pension, calculated as if he had reached 65. If he is still disabled at age 65 he receives the retirement pension calculated at the time of disability (adjusted for inflation). The children of a disabled contributor receive benefits which are comparable to the orphan's benefits.

GOVERNMENT ANNUITIES

One of the objectives of government policy towards the aged is that individuals be provided means of saving for their own retirement. The earliest program for old age pensions in Canada was designed to provide such a means. From 1908 to 1975 individuals were able to buy annuities from the government under the provisions of the Government Annuities Act. Among the various types of contracts allowed were deferred life annuities, lifetime pensions commencing at some future date. The premiums are based on mortality tables and rates of interest specified in the Act. The annuities program is in direct competition with similar investments in the private sector. According to Bryden (1974), the life insurance industry has lobbied strenuously against the Act. They have argued that the taxpayers are 'subsidizing' those who purchased the annuities because the administrative costs are not considered in calculating the benefits.[6] In fact

5 There are additional requirements for those whose contribution period exceeds 10 years.
6 CCH Canadian (1976, 2342) states that because the administrative costs are paid out of general revenue, 'the annuities program is being subsidized by the Government.'

the degree of subsidy depends on the difference between the cost of borrowing through the issuance of bonds and the cost of borrowing through the issuance of annuities, including administrative costs. This relationship has fluctuated over the years because the interest rate incorporated in the annuities benefit calculation has remained constant for extended periods of time while market interest rates have fluctuated. There are features of the annuity program that make it less attractive than similar private plans: there is no cash surrender value, and the maximum benefits are $1200 per year. The federal government discouraged sales of annuities for many years and recently suspended all sales.

Since the public annuities program offers the same basic service as private insurance companies, it is legitimate to ask if there is any need for the government to run such a program. The original justification for the Act was that people did not trust private companies with their savings (Bryden, 1974, 51-2). This problem can be resolved with government regulation or insurance of private companies operating in this area. On the other hand there is really no fundamental difference between the sale of a Canada Savings Bond and the sale of an annuity. In either case the government is a competitor of those offering private financial instruments. The only difference is that the private sector receives a commission on the sale of a savings bond. A similar arrangement could be made for annuities.

Although the annuity program is being phased out, the history of the Annuities Act offers two insights into the political climate in regard to retirement income. The first is the longstanding interest in a public plan that permits an individual to contribute towards his own retirement. It is widely believed that the Canada Pension Plan now meets this need, even though it is not voluntary and the benefits are relatively small. The second insight is that private industry groups can be expected to be a powerful lobby against the creation of a new type of government-issued financial instrument.

OLD AGE SECURITY

The basic Old Age Security payment is a demogrant to everyone over age 65, subject to certain residence requirements. The amount paid in 1975 was $1496 per person. A married couple would receive $2992. This pension is increased quarterly along with the Consumer Price Index. Old Age Security benefits are treated as taxable income.

GUARANTEED INCOME SUPPLEMENT

The Guaranteed Income Supplement is in effect a negative income tax with a guarantee of $1049 for a single individual over age 65 and a 50 per cent tax on the recipient's own income (excluding OAS benefits and provincial pensions). This means that up to $2098 in income from other sources may be received before GIS benefits equal zero. The GIS benefits are not taxable under the Income Tax Act. A married couple receive a guarantee 75 per cent larger than the guarantee for a single individual or pensioner with a younger spouse.

Effective 1 October 1975 the spouse of a pensioner became eligible for OAS and GIS benefits if he or she is between the ages of 60 and 64. Previously the spouse received no benefits until age 65. The spouse's allowance guarantees an income equal to the regular OAS benefits for a couple plus the regular GIS benefits for a married couple. The income test is somewhat more complicated. The spouse loses OAS benefits at a rate of seventy-five cents for each one dollar of the couple's income. After the OAS benefit is exhausted (at earnings of $2112 when the program began in October 1975) further income causes a loss of the couples' GIS benefits at the rate of fifty cents for each dollar in income.

GUARANTEED ANNUAL INCOME SYSTEM (GAINS)

Since 1974 Ontario has supplemented the OAS and GIS benefits for those over 65. The guarantee level in 1975 averaged $2890 for a single individual and double that for a couple. This implies a $345 payment for someone with only OAS and GIS income. GAINS 'taxes' income from other sources, including GIS, at a 100 per cent rate.

ONTARIO TAX CREDIT

Ontario has a tax credit system which also operates like a negative income tax. Tax credits are based on property taxes (or rental payments), personal exemptions, and pensioner status. The 'tax-back' rate is 2 per cent of taxable income. Since a pensioner might have as much as $5000 in income that is not taxable, the tax credit system is a negative income tax with a large tax exemption. It is, in effect, a lump sum grant for those without taxable income. Assuming that $1500 in rent is paid, a pensioner in 1975 with no taxable income would receive $210 in property tax credit, $31 in sales tax credit and $110 in pensioner tax credit. The total tax credit in this example is $351.

INCOME TAX PROVISIONS

The Income Tax Act is very generous to those receiving pension income. There is an old age exemption of $1174 in 1975 for each taxpayer and a $1000 exemption for private pension income. When the $1000 dividend and interest exemption is operative, an individual aged 65 and over would not pay taxes until his income reached $5152. This figure assumes that the taxpayer has only the standard deductions and does not take into account medical deductions and other possibilities for tax savings. Since the spouse also receives these exemptions, a retired couple could receive a combined income of $10,304 without paying income tax. This hypothetical couple would receive $2992 in Old Age Security payments and the Ontario Tax Credit, of which $110 is the pensioner tax credit. A single pensioner could receive about $12,000 in income from the CPP and private pensions before the federal and provincial income tax equalled the Old Age Security payment plus the Ontario Tax Credit.[7] A couple could receive as much as $24,000 before they paid taxes in excess of OAS benefits. The tax features described here redistribute a significant amount of income from the young to the old in a given year. The old age tax exemptions make the tax system less progressive because exemptions provide a greater tax saving for high-income individuals. In a lifetime context the distributional effects of the exemptions depend on the incidence of the off-setting taxes (largely paid by the working population).

Another tax feature affecting retirement income is the treatment of Registered Retirement Savings Plans (RRSP). The income tax deductions for pension contributions in effect postpone taxes until the retirement years (or whenever the RRSP is liquidated). The contributor gains tax advantages of three types. (1) Postponement is advantageous because it is comparable to a loan equal to the tax saving in the year in which contributions are made. (2) Income earned by the RRSP can be re-invested without immediate tax. (3) When the RRSP is liquidated, the marginal rate of taxation is likely to be lower than during the working years. The RRSP provisions tend to reduce the lifetime tax burden of those with high lifetime earnings because the tax advantages are more significant at higher marginal tax rates. Furthermore, those with low to moderate incomes will be unable to contribute significant amounts to an RRSP because of their low earnings rates and because the maximum allowable contributions are proportional to earnings.

THE INCOME-TESTED PROGRAMS

Income-tested programs complicate the analysis of the benefits received from each program. An increase in CPP benefits, for instance, may reduce benefits

7 For a taxable income of $6200 the federal and Ontario provincial tax equal $1496, the OAS benefit. Total exemptions would be $5152 including interest and pension exemptions, giving a gross income of $11,852. At this level of income Ontario tax credits would be positive, depending on occupancy cost.

received from GIS and GAINS. Figure 1 illustrates the relationship between CPP and private pension income and benefits from OAS, GIS, and GAINS for an unmarried low-income individual. The horizontal axis measures income from the CPP and private pensions while the vertical axis measures total income, including benefits from public programs. For purposes of illustration, *we assume that only those with the maximum CPP benefits receive income from other sources.* The graph shows that the first $690 of income (from the CPP in this example) is taxed at a 100 per cent rate; that is, for each dollar of income, one dollar of GAINS benefits is lost. The next $1408 is taxed at a 50 per cent rate because 50 cents in GIS benefits is lost for each additional dollar of income from other sources. The 2 per cent tax-back feature of the Ontario Tax Credit begins when taxable income exceeds zero. This feature would not become operative for the low-income individual portrayed in the graph.

The graphical example supports two conclusions concerning the CPP. First, maximum CPP benefits are small in relation to the sum of the other benefits received by a low-income person. Second, those with low retirement incomes from private sources (including pensions) will receive little net increase in retirement income from their entitlement to CPP benefits. An individual with the maximum CPP benefits in 1975 (and no other private income) would receive only $427 more income per year than an individual with no CPP benefits ($3668 compared to $3241). The distributional implications and incentive effects of this feature will be analysed in chapters seven and eight.

CONCLUSIONS

This brief description of the major programs affecting those over 65 indicates that there is no unified approach to the problem of providing retirement income. Certain of the provisions are progressive while others are regressive. The most striking characteristic of the combination of programs is that the contributory program, the CPP, provides relatively small retirement benefits in relation to the benefits available from other programs. Unless new legislation is introduced the CPP will gradually increase in importance because the benefits (and contributions) reflect real growth in earnings as well as price changes.[8] Nevertheless, we can conclude that the existing public programs do not provide means by which individuals can save for their own retirement, but they may have a significant impact on the distribution of income.

---

8 This assumes that inflation is less than 12.5 per cent per year.

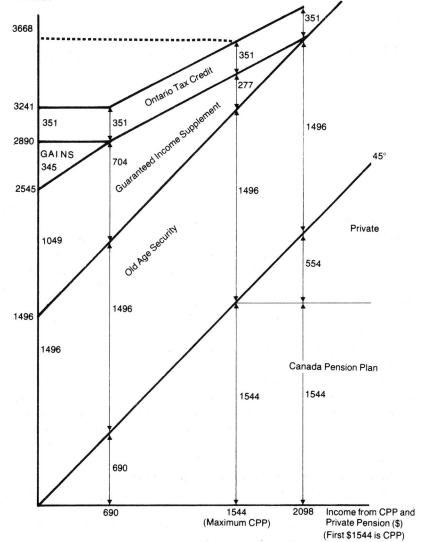

Figure 1
1975 Retirement Income

6
The financing of public pension plans

For some time economists have pointed out that there is a crucial difference between public and private pension plans (Samuelson, 1958; Aaron, 1966). Public plans need not be financed by an investment fund because the government has the power to tax those in the labour force in order to provide retirement income. Corporations may also be able to finance pension plans without an investment fund, but legislation requires that they be funded. This legislation is necessary because of the possibility of corporate bankruptcy.

Since a public pension plan may be financed out of current tax revenues, accumulated capital (an investment fund), or a combination of the two, the designers of a public pension program must choose the method of financing. Public discussion of this issue usually centres on concerns over the security of public pensions in the absence of a fund. Contrary to popular belief, the existence of an investment fund does not by itself guarantee that pension commitments will be honoured. For example, future workers could always tax away pension benefits if they desired a larger share of national income. To most economists the choice between the two methods of financing (ignoring the partially funded approach) depends not on the security of a pension backed by an investment fund but on the empirical relationship between the social rate of return on capital and the rate of growth of aggregate earnings. This criterion will be discussed in the next section.

The economic discussion which follows may seem irrelevant to today's workers, who are concerned with their own retirement. In fact, however, there is an important link between the popular concern over pension security and the economic discussion. The safety of public pensions depends on the willingness of future generations to provide the pensions that are promised today's workers. This willingness will depend on two considerations: (1) the share of national income which is required to meet the pension obligations, which in turn depends on the level of national income and the ratio of pensioners to workers, and (2) the prospects that the pension system will be perpetuated, guaranteeing that future generations will be supported during their own retirement. Both considerations suggest that the viability of the pensions promised today's workers depends on long-term economic considerations and the acceptability to future generations of the pension rules of the game which we establish.

OPTIMAL FINANCING

The question of optimal financing of social security programs was raised in a controversy between Samuelson (1958) and Lerner (1959). Samuelson sought a method which would 'give every representative man ... a lifetime consumption profile that he would prefer over any other one available to him and to everyone else' (Samuelson, 1959, 519). Lerner, on the other hand, seeks a redistribution of income which 'maximizes at each period society's total utility' (Samuelson, 1959, 521). Those who favour the Lerner approach (Asimakopulos and Weldon, 1968) argue that without an enforceable contract between current and future governments, the future implications of a retirement program cannot be considered. We do not find the Lerner argument persuasive. If today's pension program does not establish the rules of the game for tomorrow's program, there is little incentive for workers, the majority of the population, to support the aged. If, however, the working population believe that the retirement income system will be in operation when they are retired, they will wish to design the system so as to maximize their own individual lifetime utility. As further support for the notion that a retirement system will have some permanence, it is shown below that under a pay-as-you-go plan a majority of the population at any point in the future will *not* wish to reduce benefits and contributions.

The financing issue can be explained with a simple life-cycle consumption model (Feldstein, 1974b). Consider a representative consumer who must decide how much to consume and save in each of two periods. In the first period, the pre-retirement years, he works and must save in order to have income after retirement. In Figure 2 the individual earns y_1^0 during the first period, saves $y_1^0 - c_1^0$, earns a rate of return i, and is able to consume $c_2^0 = (1+i)(y_1^0 - c_1^0)$ during the second period. He chooses a point B where the budget line is tangent to an indifference curve. A program is now introduced which would tax a fraction t of the individual's earnings in order to finance a public pension plan. Assume for simplicity that $c_1^0 = (1 - t)y_1^0$, in other words the individual

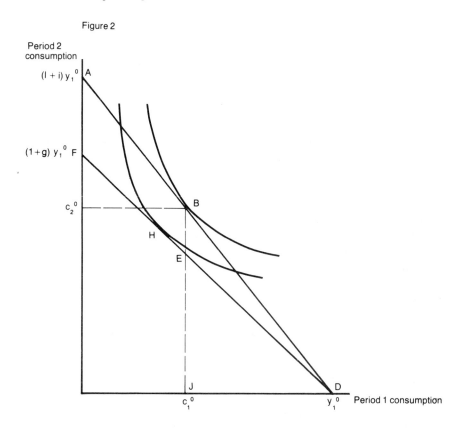

Figure 2

Period 2 consumption

$(1 + i) y_1^0$ A

$(1+g) y_1^0$ F

c_2^0 B

H

E

J

D

c_1^0

y_1^0 Period 1 consumption

consumes all of his after tax income. One must know the level of pension that can be provided with this tax. If the tax revenue is used to create an investment fund and the real rate of return is equal to i, the pension will equal $(1 + i)(t) y_1^0 = c_2^0$. The individual will find himself at point B just as before the program. The only difference is that his private saving has been completely replaced by a tax and his private pension has been replaced by a public pension.

On the other hand, if the tax revenue is used to finance current pension recipients and the plan maintains the same tax rate, the funds available for the individual's pension will grow at a rate equal to the real rate of growth of the tax base. The tax base, which is aggregate earnings, will grow by an amount equal to the growth in the labour force plus the real rate of growth of earnings per worker. Assume that real aggregate earnings grow at a rate of g per year. In Figure 2 the new tangent line DEF indicates that g is less than i. The public pension that can be provided, JE, is less than the pension provided by an investment fund. The individual is worse off because DEF falls below DBA. If g exceeds i the individual would be better off with the pay-as-you-go technique. If $i = g$ the two methods are identical.

The demonstrated optimality condition applies only after the public pension plan has been in place for a long period of time. A pay-as-you-go system will always be preferred by the first pension recipients who receive benefits without having contributed during their working years. Furthermore, a public pension that requires more saving than an individual would have voluntarily made (with the same rate of return) will be considered sub-optimal by the individual. The optimality condition implies that an investment fund will lead to real capital formation. (This point will be discussed below.)

The choice between the two methods of financing thus depends on a comparison of two empirical parameters, the real rate of interest and the real rate of growth of earnings. This comparison requires the selection of the appropriate rate of interest. It will be argued below that the appropriate measure is the *social* rate of return on capital, as opposed to the *private* rate of return. The private return is less than the social return by the amount of taxes on the returns to capital. Aggregate real wages, salaries and supplements paid in Canada grew at a 5.7 per cent rate between 1955 and 1974.[1] (The labour force grew at a 2.9 per cent annual rate, which implies a 2.8 per cent rate of growth of earnings per worker.) Jenkins (1972, 36-7) has estimated that the social rate of return on capital in Canada was 9.7 per cent during the period 1965 to 1969 (The private – after tax – rate of return was 6.3 per cent).[2] This implies that an investment fund is preferred because the social rate of return exceeds the rate of growth of aggregate earnings.[3] The reasons for the use of the social rate of return will be discussed following an explanation of the role of demographic factors in the financing decision.

1 Canada (1975a). Employment grew at a 2.8 per cent rate.
2 Excluding sales taxes and capital gains. Jenkins estimates of the private return are very close to the 5.75 real rate of return on the Toronto Stock Exchange for the 1956 to 1973 period.
3 The condition that indifference between the two financing techniques occurs when $i = g$ can be interpreted in terms of the golden rule of economic growth. When i exceeds g there is not enough saving in the economy according to the golden rule. The higher capital stock with an investment fund under this circumstance will bring the economy closer to the golden rule path.

THE IMPACT OF DEMOGRAPHIC CHANGES ON PENSION FINANCING

The growth rate of earnings depends critically on the rate of employment growth and on the rate of growth of earnings per worker. A slow-down in the rate of growth of population or in labour force participation will make a pay-as-you-go plan even less desirable. In the future Canada can expect reduced population growth if present fertility trends continue, implying that the labour force population will grow at a much slower rate. For instance, with the total fertility rate equal to 2.13 and gross immigration equal to 200,000 per year the annual rate of increase of men aged 25 to 54 will fall from 2.1 per cent in the 1971 to 2000 period to 0.6 per cent in the 2000 to 2025 period. Present fertility rates are below the 2.13 level.[4]

Increases in the labour force participation rate can offset to only a limited extent the decline in population growth. Between 1964 and 1974 the participation rate grew at an annual rate of 0.75 per cent per year. This increase is due to rising female labour force participation. If this rate of growth continued for 50 years, the participation rate would equal 78.6, roughly equal to the male participation rate in 1974 (77.3). This rate must be considered the upper limit of labour force participation, since it implies almost universal labour force participation of married women. One must conclude that the rate of growth of labour force participation, even if it is considerable, will not be sufficient to offset the decline in population growth. Furthermore, since the labour force participation rate cannot exceed 100 and is unlikely to exceed 77, any acceleration in the rate of growth of participation cannot be sustained.

Not only does a slower rate of growth of population move a pay-as-you-go system further away from optimality, it also necessitates much higher contribution rates. The ratio of the over-65 population to the working population rises dramatically in the long run when the fertility rate falls. Table 9 illustrates the implications of alternative fertility rates and immigration rates on the ratio of those 65 and over to those 14-64. This ratio will be referred to as the *pensioner ratio*. Even the least dramatic assumption concerning fertility rates and immigration (2.13 fertility rate and 200,000 immigration) produces a doubling of the pensioner ratio between 1975 and 2050, with most of the change taking place by 2025. The table indicates that only a slight increase in the ratio will take place by the year 2000, regardless of the assumption.

The pensioner ratio gives a rough indication of the tax rate necessary to finance a pay-as-you-go pension. If the proportion of those 14-64 who work

---

4 The 1973 period total fertility rate was 1.93 (Canada, 1973a, 56). The 2.13 rate is near zero population growth level with no immigration. Immigration was 218,000 in 1974.

TABLE 9

Population and ratio, age 65 and over to age 14 to 64

| Gross annual immigration | Year | Period total fertility rate | | | | | |
| | | 1.80 | | 2.13 | | 2.50 | |
		Population (million)	65+ / (14-64)	Population (million)	65+ / (14-64)	Population (million)	65+ / (14-64)
100,000	1975	22.359	0.1281	22.550	0.1281	22.765	0.1281
	2000	27.200	0.1727	29.226	0.1647	31.573	0.1566
	2025	28.590	0.2864	33.782	0.2440	40.412	0.2068
	2050	26.716	0.3090	35.984	0.2536	49.150	0.2076
200,000	1975	22.773	0.1263	22.967	0.1263	23.185	0.1263
	2000	30.745	0.1587	32.925	0.1519	35.447	0.1450
	2025	35.634	0.2597	41.448	0.2258	48.832	0.1949
	2050	36.888	0.2799	47.693	0.2367	62.867	0.1984

NOTE: Projections from 1971 population. Projection program developed by C. Cohen, Institute for Policy Analysis. Emigration assumed equal to 60,000 per year. Mortality rates from Canada (1974a).

equals the proportion of those 65 and over who are eligible for a pension, the pensioner ratio indicates the tax rate on total earnings required to provide a pension equal to the average earnings. (Note, for example that if the pensioner ratio were equal to one, the tax rate would have to be 100 per cent in order to provide a pension equal to average earnings.) If the pension is less than average earnings, the tax rate equals the pensioner ratio times the fraction of earnings paid. Table 9 indicates that current contribution rates must increase 15-35 per cent by the year 2000 and 54-124 per cent by the year 2025, depending on the population assumptions. For instance, with a 2.13 fertility rate and 200,000 immigration, contribution rates would have to increase 20 per cent by the year 2000 and 79 per cent by the year 2025 (0.2258/0.1263 = 1.79). Further increases will be required if pensions are increased relative to earnings or if an earlier retirement age is adopted. In 1971 the lowering of the ratirement age to 60 would have increased the pensioner ratio by 53 per cent, requiring a 53 per cent increase in the pay-as-you-go contribution rates.

The pensioner ratio is directly related to the choice of the optimal method of financing. If the rate of growth of the labour force equals s, the number of years of retirement equal p and the number of years in the labour force equal m, the pensioner ratio in the long run equals

$$(_{0}^{p}\int e^{st}dt)/(_{p}^{p+m}\int e^{st}dt) = (e^{sp}-1)/e^{sp}(e^{sm}-1). \tag{3}$$

As the formula indicates, the pensioner ratio is directly related to the labour force growth rate. For the individual the choice between an investment fund and a pay-as-you-go system is determined by a comparison of the capital value of the actual pension at retirement with the pension that would be received had the contributions been invested. (Aaron, 1966). The contribution rate for a pay-as-you-go system equals the pensioner ratio

$$(e^{sp} - 1)/e^{sp}(e^{sm} - 1)$$

multiplied by the ratio of the pension to average earnings, k. After m years of these contributions invested at a rate of interest i, the capital value at retirement equals:

$$e^{im}{}_{0}\int^{m}k[(e^{sp}-1)/e^{sp}(e^{sm}-1)]w_{0}e^{(h-i)t}dt = [k(e^{sp}-1)e^{im}w_{0}(e^{(h-i)m}-1)]/$$

$$e^{sp}(e^{sm}-1)(h-i), \tag{4}$$

where h is the rate of growth of real average earnings and w_0 is the initial earnings level. The pension benefit, a fraction k of average earnings, will have a capital value in the year of retirement equal to

$$\int_{m}^{m+p} (kw_0 e^{ht} dt / e^{i(t-m)}) = [e^{im} (kw_0) (e^{(h-i)(m+p)} - e^{(h-i)m})] / (h-i). \quad (5)$$

The two capital values in equations (4) and (5) will be equal if $s + h = i$, or if the rate of growth of the labour force plus the rate of growth of average earnings equals the rate of return. In other words the previously derived optimality condition continues to hold.

A slower rate of growth of the labour force, because of declining participation rates, lower fertility rates, or reduced immigration, raises the contribution rate required by a pay-as-you-go system. The slower growth raises the value of the pension that would have been received had the (increased) contributions been invested. The value of the actual pension remains unchanged because it is expressed as a fraction of average earnings. In other words, a slower rate of growth of the labour force requires more contributions from each contributor in order to finance a pay-as-you-go system, while the value of the pension remains unchanged. The result is that the investment fund method becomes preferable when the pensioner ratio rises above the critical value where the rate of growth of aggregate real earnings equals the real rate of return.

One can conclude that Canada's future population structure will almost certainly shift towards a larger ratio of pensioners to workers. Most of this shift will occur after the year 2000. In the process the rate of growth of the labour force will fall, making pay-as-you-go financing increasingly inferior to investment fund financing. Small increases in contribution rates for today's workers will eliminate the need for substantial increases in the future. If pension benefits are increased relative to average earnings or if the retirement age is lowered, there is an even greater need for an investment fund in order to avoid prohibitively high pay-as-you-go contribution rates that might jeopardize the willingness of future workers to finance the pension benefits.

DIVERGENCE OF THE SOCIAL RATE OF RETURN AND THE RATE OF SOCIAL TIME PREFERENCE

Previously it was pointed out that there are many alternative rates of interest that might be used in choosing the optimal method of financing. The social rate of return on capital estimated to be 9.7 per cent exceeds the private rate of return (6.3 per cent) in part because of corporate income taxes. The rate of return on less risky assets such as government bonds will be even lower than the return on private investment. For example, the real rate of return on long-term Government of Canada bonds approximated 2.5 per cent during the 1958 to 1974 period.[5] Rational pension contributors will evaluate the stream of benefits and contributions using a rate of discount similar to the after tax return on government bonds. This is the rate of social time preference for relatively riskless future consumption. (Feldstein, 1974c). Since the rate of growth of real aggregate earnings (5.7 per cent) has exceeded the rate of return on bonds, one might think that pay-as-you-go financing should be preferred. It turns out that the basic conclusion concerning the method of financing is not altered by the multitude of rates of return and the empirical fact that the rate of growth of aggregate earnings lies between the social rate of return and the market rate of return for government securities. (The after tax rate of time preference is even smaller.) The implications of the relationship between these rates of return will be discussed as will the suggestion (Feldstein, 1976b) that a pension fund should pay the social rate of return.

The choice of financing will be considered first under the life cycle saving model. If a pension offers an after tax rate of return (r) which equals the rate of time preference and the after tax return on alternative investments, the pension plan will reduce private saving by the amount of the contributions. If there is an investment fund, total saving and investment will remain unchanged. If there is a pay-as-you-go plan and beneficiaries consume all their income, saving and investment will fall by the amount of the contribution. The social rate of return (s) reflects the opportunity cost of this investment to society. The pension plan appears to offer the same return in this example regardless of the method of financing, but for society there is a reduction in future income because of the decrease in investment. In fact this loss of income outweighs the return offered by the pension under a pay-as-you-go system since s exceeds r. Although the pension recipient may earn a rate of return r the decline in investment eliminates

5 No data exist in Canada which actually compare the realized return (i.e., interest return plus (minus) the capital gain (loss) on the bond) on bonds with the rate of inflation for alternative holding periods. Even if such data were available, one could only infer *ex ante* real rates of return by decomposing realized inflation into its expected and unexpected components. The figure cited in the text was obtained simply by comparing the average interest rate on long-term (ten-year and over) Government of Canada bonds with the average rate of inflation, measured by the Consumer Price Index, for the period 1958-74. To the extent that inflation, on average, during this period was underestimated, the (non-observable) *ex ante* real return on long-term Government of Canada bonds would be higher than the 2.5 per cent real rate employed in the calculations in the text. Recalculation of this figure with a synthetic price expectations series (see Appendix A) does not materially alter the result.

his share of the taxes on the returns to the investment. These taxes account for the difference between the social rate of return and the rate of social time preference. As long as the rate of growth of earnings is less than the social rate of return, the investment fund method is preferred.[6]

If contributors base their consumption decisions on current disposable income, the decision to finance by an investment fund will produce an increase in investment and the stock of capital. The pay-as-you-go alternative will simply transfer consumption goods from workers to pensioners, assuming that both groups have the same marginal propensity to consume. One is led to the same conclusion as above. The social rate of return is used for the comparison because the investment method leads to greater real investment.

Feldstein (1974b) argues that the pension fund could be supplemented with general tax revenue to bring the rate of return for the fund up to the social rate of return. If the rate of return in the pension exceeds the market rate of return, the members of the pension plan who behave according to the life cycle model will reduce their saving and increase their consumption because of the wealth effect. This is precisely what Feldstein (1974a) found in the US (see chapter eight). If a return in excess of the rate of time preference is paid, the capital stock will be reduced in spite of the investment fund.[7]

What happens to capital formation if a Keynesian consumption function is more appropriate than a life cycle consumption function? If consumption and saving depend solely on current disposable income, the rate of return implicit in the pension fund is immaterial. A transfer of tax revenue to pensioners in order to supplement the difference between the market return earned by the pension fund and the social rate of return will have no effect on consumption and investment.[8] Ironically, the suggestion that the pension pay the social rate of return is appropriate only if the life cycle consumption model does not apply.

One can conclude that the decision to have an investment fund should be based on a comparison of the rate of growth of earnings with the social rate of return. However, the contributions should be set so that they cover future

---

6 The first generation to receive benefits without contributing will prefer the pay-as-you-go method. Subsequent generations will prefer the investment fund.
7 If the rate of growth of aggregate earnings is already less than the social rate of return, the decreased investment will move the economy further away from a 'golden rule' consumption path.
8 This assumes that the marginal propensity to consume is the same for pensioners and workers. If the revenue would have been spent for government goods and services and the marginal propensity to consume of pensioners is one, resources are shifted from government to private consumption.

liabilities when the fund is accumulated at the market rate of interest. Any higher rate of return will reduce total capital formation.

CANADA PENSION PLAN FINANCING

The Canada Pension Plan is nominally financed on an investment fund basis. The revenue which has been collected from employers' and employees' contributions goes into a fund which by the end of 1974 had a value of 7.9 billion dollars. (Canada, 1974b, 1). The fund purchases provincial securities in relation to the provinces' contributions. For instance, in fiscal year 1975-6 Ontario (1975a, c-8) expected to borrow $750 million from the CPP. The rate charged the provinces is the Government of Canada rate for securities with a term to maturity of 20 years or more.

An important issue is whether or not the CPP is in fact financed on an investment fund basis. This issue in turn has two dimensions: (1) the extent to which the CPP is actuarially sound, and (2) the extent to which the accumulated fund in fact serves to finance investment. The first problem is that the level of contributions is insufficient to cover future benefits, despite the existence of a fund. The Department of Insurance (Canada, 1973b, 11), for example, estimates that the fund will reach a peak in 1990 and decline to zero between the years 1995 and 2000 (see Table 10.) This estimate implies that the CPP is only partially funded. Contributions are insufficient to cover future benefits at market rates of return. The contributions will have to be increased in the future to cover the then current benefits, but if the past is any indication, future contributions will probably lag behind the level necessary to completely cover liabilities.[9]

Even if the fund were sufficient to cover future benefits, one could not necessarily conclude that the CPP had an investment fund in a meaningful sense. As noted previously, all of the CPP funds are invested in provincial securities. This fact does not alter the previous conclusions regarding the impact of the CPP on the aggregate level of savings, so long as the availability of CPP funds does *not* lead to an increase in current expenditure by the provincial governments. For the moment, assume that the marginal propensity to consume is unity for CPP contributors. Any increase in contributions without an increase in current benefits will thus lead to reduced consumption. Assume that the economy is

9 According to the advisory committee of the Canada Pension Plan (Canada, 1975b, 2-6), the Plan was originally intended to be financed on a pay-as-you-go basis. A partly funded plan resulted because Quebec had already designed a funded plan. See also Simeon (1972).

TABLE 10

Canada, Department of Insurance, CPP projections

Calendar year	Benefits and expenses (million $)	Contributions (million $)	Cash flow to provinces (million $)	Fund (billion $)
1973				6.6
1974	466	1105	639	7.7
1975	615	1255	640	8.9
1976	814	1385	572	10.1
1977	1037	1536	499	11.4
1978	1285	1696	411	12.6
1979	1555	1878	323	13.8
1980	1844	2039	196	15.0
1981	2127	2216	89	16.1
1982	2430	2400	−30	17.2
1983	2753	2592	−161	18.2
1984	3101	2793	−308	19.1
1985	3476	3003	−473	19.9
1990	5845	4208	−1637	21.3
1995	9028	5808	−3220	14.9
2000	13,178	8115	−5063	−4.1
2005	18,679	11,425	−7254	−41.7
2010	26,678	15,899	−10,780	−109.5
2015	39,631	21,719	−17,912	−233.8
2020	58,863	29,321	−29,542	−459.3
2025	86,732	39,460	−47,272	−854.9

SOURCE: Canada (1973b, 11)
NOTE: Assumptions: growth of earnings 5.5 per cent, interest rate 6.5 per cent, rate of inflation 3 per cent

maintained at full employment through the use of monetary policy.[10] Assume also that the supply of public securities is constant. Consider what would happen if the CPP fund invested in *both* public and private securities, purchased in the market place. The annual revenue surplus of the fund would constitute saving by the economy, and this saving would be channelled into the capital market. The increased supply of funds would drive down the interest rate and stimulate

10 Carroll (1960) analyses the implications of a reserve fund without allowing for effective monetary policy.

increased real investment. The public would be forced to save in the form of CPP contributions, and in a real sense the fund would be investing in the economy.

Now consider what would happen if the CPP fund purchased only provincial bonds in the market. The increased demand for provincial bonds would lower the rate of return on provincial bonds and thus increase the private sector's purchases of other securities. The net result would be the same as before, with increased real investment in the private sector. The private sector would hold relatively fewer provincial bonds than if the CPP purchased all types of securities.

Note that the requirement that the CPP fund purchase only provincial securities does raise potential problems. Knowing that the CPP fund has to invest a given amount in provincial securities, a province could offer bonds at a very low rate of interest, even a negative rate of interest, without fear of reducing the demand for bonds below a certain level. Therefore, the purchases of provincial securities must be tied to a market rate. In practice the federal 20-year bond rate on outstanding issues has been used as the rate for the purchase of provincial securities. The CPP advisory committee has claimed that this rate is 1.12 to 1.65 percentage points below the provincial market rate (Canada, 1975b, 28). This estimated difference reflects the higher risk class for provincial bonds and the premium that is paid for the low coupon federal bonds.[11] The added underwriting costs for market issues should be added to the subsidy to the provinces.[12] The advisory committee does not point out that the return on CPP investments could be higher if the fund managers were free to invest in any security. Another implication of this argument is that provincial bond rates would be much higher than the current market rate without purchases by the CPP. The increased rates would result from a greater supply in the market and the possibility that the bonds might fall into a higher risk category.

The optimality of an investment fund hinged on an assumption that the funds led to real investment. If the funds are used to increase current government expenditure at the provincial level, contributions are just like any other tax. If the economy is already at full employment, an increase in taxes and expenditures on goods and services will divert output from private consumption to public consumption. If the expenditures occur in the form of transfers, consumption goods are redistributed among individuals. Real investment occurs whenever capital is created, whether human or non-human. If no real investment

11 Part of the return for low coupon bonds is taxed as capital gains. New long-term issues with higher coupon values would yield a higher return.
12 An Ontario document (Ontario, 1976) argues that the rate should be lower than the market rate because the bonds are recallable at par value, implying no risk of capital loss. This is a pointless argument because the bonds will not be recalled until the provincial cash flow becomes sufficiently negative.

is made, future benefits are entirely paid out of future taxes, and in effect the program becomes a pay-as-you-go pension plan combined with a payroll tax used to finance government expenditure. On the other hand, if the increased provincial expenditure is for investment, the flow of services generated by the investment will benefit future taxpayers, who in effect pay for the services through interest payment to the CPP. In order for investment fund financing to be optimal when government investment is financed by the fund, the investment must yield the social rate of return. This is not always the case with government investments.

There are, however, several reasons why the provinces might increase their expenditure when the CPP purchases their bonds. The first reason is that the average interest rate on provincial bonds decreases because they are sold at the federal rate. The marginal rate will also be lower because of the decreased supply of provincial bonds in the market. If the provincial deficit is large, the implicit reduction in marginal cost may be considerable. The lower interest cost may induce more current consumption of government goods and services as opposed to future consumption. An even greater increase in expenditure might take place if the provinces feel that they will never have to pay back the loan from the CPP fund. There are a number of observers who feel that this is the case. (Bird, 1976). Public statements by the Ontario government imply that CPP-owned debt is treated differently than publically-held debt (Ontario, 1974, 26-7). As pointed out above, if the contributions are used for additional current expenditures, the CPP is basically a regressive payroll tax used to finance government expenditure, including current CPP benefits.[13]

To highlight the issues, assume that the CPP pension fund buys Government of Canada bonds. Assume also that the CPP contributions have no affect on consumption, as suggested by the life cycle model, and that full employment is maintained by monetary policy. If the revenue from the sale of bonds is not used to increase current expenditure, private investment will remain unchanged.[14] Canada Bonds are now held indirectly by CPP contributors rather than the original bond holders. If the government undertakes additional investment, current production is channeled from private investment into government investment. Future taxpayers will enjoy the services provided by the capital acquired and tax revenue will be used to pay back the loan from previous taxpayers. If the revenue from the sale of bonds is used for additional current

13 The contributions are regressive because of the ceiling on contributions and the fact that the contributions are tax deductible.
14 This assumes that the contributions do not exceed the prior savings rate.

government expenditure, goods and services are diverted from private investment to government services by the resulting rise in interest rates. Future tax-payers will have to pay back the loan from retired tax-payers without receiving the benefits resulting from a greater capital stock. One way to finance the repayment is with CPP contributions. In effect an investment fund which is used to finance increased current government expenditure is equivalent to pay-as-you-go financing. Similarly, an investment fund which leads to government investment with a rate of return that is less than the rate of growth of earnings will be inferior to pay-as-you-go financing.

The assumption that consumption does not respond to increased pension contributions implies a life cycle consumption model. In a world in which the wage earners base their consumption on current disposable income, pension contributions will reduce consumption. If government bonds are purchased with the funds and the government does not increase its expenditures, private investment will increase as the interest rate falls. The pension contributions will have resulted in increased investment and an increased capital stock. If the government increases its capital expenditure, government investment replaces private consumption and private investment. If additional government expenditure for current consumption exceeds the reduction in private consumption (the marginal propensity to consume is less than one), the capital stock will fall because of the decline in private investment. As in the case of life cycle consumption behaviour the implications of financing with an investment fund which purchases government securities depend on the extent to which (1) government expenditures increase because of the availability of revenue and (2) the additional government expenditures are used for transfers, purchases of goods and services for current consumption, or for investment that yields the social rate of return.

There is really no way to test whether or not the CPP investment arrangements have affected provincial expenditure. Foot (1975) has tested several models of provincial expenditure, but the predictive power of the models is not sufficient to give an adequate test of the effects of the CPP. Foot's data do show, however, that the real expenditure per capita in Ontario has increased substantially since 1965. Whether or not this is due to the CPP funds which became available in 1966 cannot be determined. In recent years Ontario has been able to retire a substantial amount of publically-held debt because of the increased CPP debt, but total debt has increased (Foot, 1975, 55). In other provinces some CPP funds have gone to crown corporations which might otherwise have had to borrow in the marketplace.

A recent Province of Ontario study (Ontario, 1976) illustrates how the provinces might attempt to eliminate the debt to the CPP. In the absence of a fully funded system, the study appears to favour a pay-as-you-go plan in which current contributions are used to cover current benefits plus expenses. The interest received by the existing fund is simply accumulated. Interest paid by the provinces on existing debt would be used by the fund to purchase new provincial debt. Although the CPP fund would continue to grow, this scheme could amount to forgiveness of the existing debt. An alternative method of financing is one in which the provinces must borrow publicly in order to meet interest payments, which are used to finance benefits. The preference revealed in the Ontario study suggests, at the very least, that an accumulation of provincial obligations by the CPP fund is preferable to an accumulation of provincial obligations by the public. If this view is in fact held by the Province of Ontario, an increase in provincial expenditure in response to current CPP purchases of provincial obligations is not unlikely.

CONCLUSIONS

Economic theory suggests that investment fund financing is optimal for the CPP using Samuelson's optimality criterion. The optimality of investment fund financing will become even more obvious when lower fertility rates ultimately produce lower growth rates for the labour force and a higher ratio of pensioners to workers. In the current institutional setting, investment fund financing creates a new source of provincial revenue that might lead to increased expenditure for transfers or current government services. If government investment takes place, the rate of return may be less than the return in the private sector. The current institutional setting may preclude the establishment of an investment fund in the economic sense of the term. If this is the case, the pay-as-you-go method may be perferable to a system that finances increased provincial expenditure with a regressive payroll tax.

The provinces are going to find that the cash flow from the CPP fund will become small even if an investment fund is created because of the projected slow-down in labour force growth. Ultimately new debt financing for the provinces will have to come from the capital market. Therefore, the provinces must sooner or later become independent of the CPP fund for new financing. The payment of market rates of interest may serve to emphasize the nature of the provincial obligation to the fund and deter additional expenditure. In addition, the CPP should follow Quebec's example by purchasing private securities with the CPP funds. This institutional arrangement would prevent additional CPP contributions from financing current government expenditures.

Provided that the changes described above can be made, the optimality of investment fund financing suggests that current contribution rates should be increased to a level sufficient to cover future benefits under the CPP program. The next chapter will consider whether or not distributional effects might influence the financing decision.

7
Distributional impact of Canada's retirement income programs

A program as complex as the Canada Pension Plan must invariably redistribute income among different members of society. Some economists believe that the primary objective of a pension is to redistribute income between generations (Asimakopulos and Weldon, 1970). A pension play may cause other types of redistribution, such as between income classes and between sexes. In this chapter the nature of the redistribution implicit in the Canada Pension Plan will be examined, and the role of the Guaranteed Income Supplement and Ontario's GAINS program will also be considered.

ISSUES IN THE ANALYSIS OF REDISTRIBUTION

What is meant by the redistributive effect of the pension program? There is some disagreement in the economic literature concerning how one defines distribution in the case of a pension program. There are at least four main problems inherent in the analysis. First, should the distributional effect of benefits and contributions be analysed separately or as a package? Second, what is the incidence of the employer's contribution? Third, how does one define equity? Fourth, should the distribution effects be analysed independently of other income-tested programs, such as the Guaranteed Income Supplement in Canada? These issues will be discussed in turn.

Distribution of benefits and contributions
There are two ways of analysing a public pension plan. One can consider such a plan either as a transfer program for the aged financed by a payroll tax, or as a

compulsory savings program. The public appears to adopt the latter view of the CPP. Many people feel that the relationship between contributions (by employer and employee) and benefits is roughly equivalent to the relationship that might hold in a private pension plan or a life insurance scheme. One can easily see why this view is not necessarily correct. There is no contractual obligation on the part of the government to maintain benefits and contributions at their present level, and the government's powers of taxation and borrowing free the CPP of any need to be 'actuarially sound.' Brittain (1972, 83) summarized this view: 'Since any benefit levels can be financed by a variety of tax structures, the latter invite comparison in their own right.'[1]

On the other hand an argument can be made that because members of the public believe that they are accumulating their own retirement fund, it would be politically impossible to make a change in the structure of the Act. This view implies that the variety of politically feasible tax structures may be limited, because the public support for the CPP may be entirely derived from the fact that contributions and benefits are linked. To say that any tax structure could be used to finance benefits does not alter the fact that there exists a particular structure. One is interested in the effect of the existing structure of taxes and benefits over a lifetime. For example, it makes little sense to argue that the benefit structure is regressive if those who receive the largest benefits make the greatest contributions. Any study of the distribution effects of the program will have to assume that the program structure will be unchanged in the future. Although modifications will be made, the effects of future changes cannot be understood unless one understands the distributional implications of the present program.

In a recent article Browning (1975) offers another justification for examining the taxes and benefits simultaneously. The welfare cost of a program (the output loss resulting from the price distorting effects of taxes and transfers) depends on the relationship between revenues and expenditures. For instance, a public pension program that offers a market rate of return on contributions and does not increase saving will have no welfare costs.[2] If the program redistributes income, it will affect individual saving and work behaviour and impose a welfare cost.[3]

---

1 Brittain argues at many points in his study that taxes and benefits should be considered separately, but goes on to consider the lifetime impact of the US social security system.
2 This assumes that the pension is a liquid asset.
3 A welfare cost in fact usually exists whether or not saving and labour supply are altered.

Those who advocate analytical separation of the contributions and benefits are particularly concerned about the regressive payroll taxes which are used to finance pensions. Brittain (1972, 153) states, 'the tenuous relationship between individual taxes and benefits does n⌐t exempt the payroll tax from the criticism that it is regressive and a heavy burden on low-income groups.' This is a narrow view of redistribution, one that considers short-run rather than life-time income. Furthermore, two separate issues seem to be lumped together: (1) the extent of lifetime redistribution and (2) the amount of forced saving. Brittain (1972, 83) argues that 'a young worker in the poverty range is not likely to be captivated by the thought that he is being forced to save in preparation for retirement while the payroll tax is pushing him deeper into poverty today.' This statement reminds us that forced saving can make someone worse off and that the poor are the most likely group to experience forced saving. This statement also implies that greater redistribution to the poor may be desirable. This redistribution may take the form of greater benefits or lower contributions. It seems reasonable to separate the redistribution issue from the forced saving issue. For the moment we are interested in the effect of the program on life-time income (or more precisely wealth) not on whether it forces someone to defer his consumption.

The incidence of employer contributions
The Canada Pension Plan is financed with contributions by both employer and employee. Slightly more than 50 per cent of the contributions for the CPP are paid by the employers.[4] This does not mean that employers bear the burden of the tax. In economic terms the incidence of the employer's contribution may fall on the employees rather than the owners of firms. This would occur if real wages were reduced by the amount of the employer's contributions. Brittain (1972) analysed the incidence of the payroll tax and concluded that the evidence supports the hypothesis that employees bear the entire burden of payroll taxes (see also Feldstein, 1974d). This conclusion will be accepted for the purpose of calculating the distributional effects of the CPP. The distributional effects will be calculated as if the individual makes all of the contributions attributable to his earnings.

Definitions of equity for a multi-period transfer program
What is the appropriate concept of equity for a program that involves payments over an extended period and benefits sometime in the future? For any

---

4 More than half is paid by employers because employees may obtain a refund for contributions in excess of the maximum and contributions paid on earnings below the annual minimum.

multi-period stream of payments one can calculate the present value at some rate of interest or the internal rate of return (the rate of interest at which the net present value equals zero). In many cases one stream might have a higher net present value than another, but a lower internal rate of return. There is no agreement in the economics literature on which concept is preferred for use in evaluating the distribution from a pension program. It is argued below that the present value approach is more reasonable. In addition to the present value versus internal rate of return issue, the concepts of progressivity and regressivity must be redefined in this context.

Brittain (1972) evaluated the US social security system using the internal rate of return.[5] He found that the rates of return were higher for those with low incomes, implying that the system is progressive. This method of evaluation avoids the difficulty of selecting a rate of interest, but the method does not make economic sense. The issue will be illustrated with a simple example. Suppose that there are two individuals, A who contributes $100 this year and receives $120 in benefits next year and B who contributes $1000 this year and receives $1100 next year. The internal rate of return is 20 per cent for A and 10 per cent for B. Is A better off than B as a result of the program? Assume that the market rate of interest is 5 per cent. The net present value of the program for A is $14.29 while the net present value for B is $47.62.[6] The program has increased B's wealth by $47.62 and A's wealth by $14.29. It seems clear that the program has benefited B more than A. After all it is an individual's wealth, the present value of his lifetime income, that determines how much consumption he can enjoy during his lifetime. The same principle should be used in evaluating educational expenditures. Someone who receives a large implicit subsidy for graduate education may earn a lower rate of return on his own investment than someone with an elementary school education, but the amount of wealth transferred may be significantly higher for the person receiving graduate training.

The present value principle can be illustrated in still another way. Consider Browning's proposal that each person contributing to a pension plan be given a government bond that earns interest equal to the rate of growth in the economy (Browning, 1973, 232). If the bonds can be traded and the market rate of interest is lower than the rate of growth, the bonds will sell for more than their par value. All contributors will receive a capital gain which represents an addition to their wealth. Suppose that some individuals contribute more than others. They will receive a larger capital gain and a greater increase in wealth. The yields on the contributions are the same for all individuals, but the pension favours those who are able to make more contributions.

5 Atkinson (1970) used the same approach. Prest (1970) calculates present values.
6 $-100 + (120/1.05) = 14.29; - 1000 + (1100/1.05) = 47.62.$

The example also illustrates the forced saving issue. If purchase of the bonds is mandatory and the bonds cannot be sold, some individuals, particularly those with low incomes, may be forced to save more than otherwise. Their wealth is higher than without the pension program, but they are forced to postpone some consumption. If society does not want to encourage postponement of consumption, sale of the bonds (or borrowing against future benefits in a more conventional scheme) can easily be permitted. This illustrates that the distribution issue can be separated from the effect of mandatory saving.

Having concluded that present value is the appropriate approach for measuring redistribution in a multi-period context, we must redefine 'progressive' and 'regressive.' Habib and Lerman (1976) also advocate the net present value of a pension program as a basis for an analysis of redistribution. They define 'excess revenues' to be the 'extra dollars' that the beneficiary receives 'above what he would have received if his tax payments had earned the market rate of return' (Habib and Lerman, 1976, 8). These excess revenues are directly related to the net present value of the pension. Excess revenues are positive if the internal rate of return exceeds the market rate of return. Habib and Lerman argue that equity is achieved if the excess revenues are distributed equally. Others might argue that equity requires an equal percentage increase in wealth for all contributors or an equal after-tax increase in wealth. This study will refer to programs as regressive if the amount of wealth transferred increases with permanent income and progressive if the amount of wealth transferred falls as permanent income increases. (The wealth will be evaluated net of taxes.)[7] The definitions of progressivity and regressivity in this context are arbitrary.

Pension plans and income maintenance programs
In the previous section it was stated that the CPP will be evaluated net of income taxes deducted for contributions and taxes paid on benefits. This approach implies that the CPP is added to an existing tax system. Should this principle be extended to include the Guaranteed Income Supplement? As explained in chapter five, additions to CPP benefits will be 'taxed' at a 50 per cent rate by the GIS plan. In Ontario GAINS taxes CPP benefits at 100 per cent rate.

The distributional effects of the CPP can be analysed in three alternative ways. First, the CPP can be evaluated as if the other programs did not exist. Second, the CPP can be analysed as if it were added to a system that included GIS and GAINS. Third, the CPP can be evaluated along with the other programs and their

7 By this definition Old Age Security, a flat payment to each person over 65, is progressive because it is taxed progressively. The old age income tax examption reduces this progressivity.

methods of financing. Each of these alternatives has different implications for the distributional effect of the CPP.

With the first approach the CPP benefits are evaluated independently. While the results are of some interest they could be misleading because those with low CPP benefits are also eligible for GIS and GAINS benefits. Alternatively one might take into account the loss of GIS and GAINS benefits when CPP benefits increase. This second approach implies that low income workers will receive no net benefits when they contribute to the CPP because there is a 100 per cent tax on CPP benefits. Finally, one might consider all of the retirement income provisions as a package. The difficulty with this approach is that the incidence of the taxes used to finance OAS, GIS, and GAINS is not known.

In this study the first approach will be used. The CPP will be evaluated without simultaneously considering the effect on other benefits. This approach is justified because the GIS and GAINS programs were designed to be supplements for those with low CPP benefits. Ideally, however, we would evaluate all government transfers simultaneously.

CPP RETIREMENT BENEFITS – THE SIMPLE CASE

The CPP retirement benefit calculations obscure the answers to a number of questions which might be asked about the program: (1) What is the effect of inflation on the level of real benefits? (2) How do the net benefits vary by income level? (3) How do the benefits depend on a worker's lifetime income profile? (4) How would the net benefits be distributed if the plan were actuarially sound? (5) What are the distributive implications of the transitional years as the program comes into maturity? These issues will be analysed by first examining the retirement benefit provision of the CPP program. A number of simplifying assumptions are made in order to clarify the issues. Later in this chapter the results of a computer simulation of the CPP are presented. In the simulations all of the details of the CPP program are taken into account.

The distributional implications of the CPP retirement benefits can be analysed by calculating the net present value of the benefits minus contributions for those with alternative income levels. If the contributions into the CPP are invested in a fund earning a real rate of return R per year, what level of retirement benefits could be financed? How does this benefit level compare with the actual benefits? These questions are answered implicitly when we consider the present value of the stream of contributions paid from age 18 to retirement age and the present value of the benefits received from retirement age onward.

Consider first someone whose earnings are always less than the YMPE. The present value of the contributions (including the employer's contribution) from age 18 to 65 is

$$C = \int_0^{47} .036(w_o e^{(G'+P)t} - YBE_o e^{(G+P)t}) e^{(-M-R-P)t} dt, \tag{6}$$

where w_o = annual earnings at age 18; G' = annual rate of growth of individual's earnings; P = rate of inflation; G = annual rate of growth of average earnings; M = annual probability of death; R = real rate of discount; YBE_o = year's basic exemption at age 18. The use of a constant probability of death for the years 18 to 65 is obviously incorrect, but it makes the calculations much simpler. A further simplifying assumption is that the YBE grows at the same rate as average earnings, which is only true after the YMPE catches up to average earnings.

For simplicity assume that the average YMPE (YMPE averaged for three years, including the year of retirement) is equal to the YMPE in the year prior to retirement and ignore the drop out provisions in the benefit calculation. Assume also that earnings are always below the YMPE. At age 65 the *annual* retirement benefit will be

$$\text{Benefits} = [.25 YMPE_o e^{46(G+P)} / 47] \int_0^{47} [w_o e^{(G'+P)t} /$$
$$YMPE_o e^{(G+P)t}] dt, \tag{7}$$

where $YMPE_o$ = year's maximum pensionable earnings at age 18. Note that if the *individual's* rate of growth of earnings (G') equals the rate of growth of *average* earnings (G), the retirement benefits equal 25 per cent of his earnings in the year prior to retirement.

The present value of the retirement benefits received from age 65 on is

$$B = [.25 YMPE_o e^{46(G+P)} D(R) / 47 e^{47(R+P)}]$$
$$\int_0^{47} [w_o e^{(G'+P)t} / YMPE_o e^{(G+P)t}] dt \tag{8}$$

where $D(R)$ = the present value of a \$1.00 life annuity at age 65 indexed for inflation.

The net present value of benefits and contributions equals

$$B-C = [D(R)(.25) e^{(46G-47R-P)} / 47] \int_0^{47} w_o e^{(G'-G)t} dt$$
$$- \int_0^{47} .036(w_o e^{(G'-M-R)t} - YBE_o e^{(G-M-R)t}) dt. \tag{9}$$

The first thing to notice about the net present value is that for the most part it does not depend on the rate of inflation. The rate of inflation enters the first term because the YMPE is averaged for a three-year period at the time of retirement. Because of the lag a higher rate of inflation lowers the real value of benefits. Inflation in the last few years prior to retirement increases contributions but is not fully built into the retirement pension calculation. Since the inflation during a three-year period is small in relation to the inflation over a life-time, for practical purposes the plan can be considered to be fully indexed. This was not true during the first few years of the plan, but recent inflation provided the impetus for nearly complete indexation.

The statement that the plan is indexed does not mean that inflation has no effect on its net present value. It is possible that an individual's real rate of growth of earnings is lower (or higher) during a period of inflation or that the real rate of discount is affected by the rate of inflation. This latter issue was discussed in chapter three where it was concluded that price expectations are incorporated in the nominal rate of return.

The next question to ask is whether the net present value increases as the initial annual earnings level increases. Differentiating the net benefits (equation 9) with respect to initial earnings gives the following:

$$\partial(B-C)/\partial w_0 = [D(R)(.25)e^{(46G-47R-P)}/47] \int_0^{47} e^{(G'-G)t}dt - \int_0^{47} .036e^{(G'-M-R)t}dt. \tag{10}$$

The net benefits increase with earnings if net benefits are sufficiently positive.[8] If net benefits are negative they become more negative as earnings increase. This implies that the retirement benefits alone may favour those with higher earnings. This conclusion might be altered when the effects of the drop out provisions and the other benefits are simulated.

Since the formula used to calculate retirement benefits does not vary with the rate of discount, the net benefits are unlikely to equal zero. In fact benefits increase with the earnings level. The common sense explanation for this characteristic is that a plan that offers a higher return than alternative investments, that is, the net present value is positive, will offer the largest wealth increase to those who are able to contribute the most. Conversely if the plan offers a lower rate of return than alternative investments, that is, the net present value is negative, it will cause the greatest wealth reduction for those who are forced to contribute the most.

It is useful to consider whether the CPP pension could be 'actuarially sound,' that is, to have net benefits equal to zero. An examination of equation (10)

8 Positive net benefits are not sufficient to guarantee that $\partial(B - C)/\partial w > 0$. Net benefits must exceed $\int_0^{47} .036YBE_0 e^{(G-M-R)t}dt.$

indicates that the net benefits can equal zero for only one wage rate, $\overline{W}$. At higher wage rates the net benefits will be negative and at lower wage rates they will be positive. At the wage where net benefits equal zero, net benefits fall if the wage rate increases:

$$\partial(B-C)/\partial w_o = -\int_0^{47} (.036YBE_o e^{(G-M-R)t} dt)/\overline{W}. \tag{11}$$

What happens if the Year's Basic Exemption (YBE) is changed? Equation 10 indicates that the rate of change of net benefits is independent of YBE. If YBE is increased, the net benefits will rise by the same amount at all earnings levels. However, if the contribution rate is simultaneously raised in order to make the plan actuarially sound, those with lower earnings will receive greater net benefits. The exception occurs when someone earns less than the YBE and therefore does not qualify for contributions or benefits.

There is some evidence that those with greater investment in human capital have a higher rate of growth of earnings (Thurow, 1969). This means that those with lower life-time earnings are relatively better off initially, but experience less growth in earnings. Because the plan averages earnings without regard to the timing of contributions, it might be better to have one's highest earnings later in life so that in effect contributions are postponed. It turns out that this is not necessarily true. If two individuals have equal lifetime earnings (defined in present value terms) but one has earnings later in his life, their net benefits can be shown to be equal if the real rate of discount (R) equals the real rate of growth of average earnings (G). The latter affects the rate of growth of YMPE. If G exceeds R it is possible, depending on the actual values of the parameters, that the person with the flatter earnings profile is better off. This possibility arises because the averaging in the benefit calculation puts relatively less weight on later earnings when G exceeds R.

The CPP may have had some redistributional effects associated with the start of the program. In the first ten years retirement benefits were reduced by a factor equal to the number of years in the contribution period (since 1966) divided by ten. Thereafter, full benefits were payable. For those retiring after 1975 it is clear that the plan is most generous for earlier cohorts. Those retiring in 1976 receive the greatest net benefits because their contribution period is only ten years. Furthermore, as the plan matures and contribution rates are increased later cohorts will lose net benefits.

In the first years of the plan the benefits were not fully indexed, but assuming that they were, those retiring in N years after 1966 receive net benefits equal to

$$[D(R)(.25)e^{(N-1)G-NR-P}/10] \int_0^N w_0 e^{(G'-G)t} dt$$
$$- \int_0^N .036 [w_0 e^{(G'-M-R)t} - YBE_0 e^{(G-M-R)t}] dt. \tag{12}$$

Differentiating with respect to N gives

$$[D(R)(.25)(G-R)e^{(N-1)G-NR-P}/10] \int_0^N w_0 e^{(G'-G)t} dt$$
$$+ [D(R)(.25)e^{(N-1)G-NR-P}/10] w_0 e^{(G'-G)N}$$
$$- .036 [w_0 e^{(G'-M-R)N} - YBE_0 e^{(G-M-R)N}]. \tag{13}$$

The sign of the above expression cannot be determined for general cases, but assuming that $M = 0, P = 0, G' = G = R, D(R) = 10$, it equals $.25 w_0 e^{-G} - .036 (w_0 - YBE_0)$ which is positive and relatively large. It seems likely that the net benefits increase with the length of contribution period for the first ten years, reach a peak for those retiring in 1976, and decline thereafter. This tendency is reinforced if the contribution rate is increased in the future with no change in the retirement benefit formula. On the other hand increased longevity will offset this tendency, and provisions for dropping out low earnings years are just coming into effect in 1976. Higher average real earnings of later cohorts will also result in higher net benefits.

Analysis becomes somewhat more complicated when taxes are considered. Benefits are taxed and contributions are allowed as a deduction. This should lower both the cost and the benefits by the same percentage if the marginal tax rate remains unchanged. To the extent that benefits exceed costs, net benefits are lower for those with higher tax rates. Since the marginal tax rate is likely to be much lower during retirement, the over-all reduction in net benefits caused by the tax system may not be very large.

In summary, the basic retirement benefit provisions will redistribute wealth to lower income individuals if the plan as a whole is actuarially sound. If net benefits are sufficiently positive, the plan is regressive. Those retiring in 1976 are likely to receive the highest net benefits from the plan, but this conclusion could be altered when 'drop-out' provisions are included.

SIMULATION OF THE CANADA PENSION PLAN

The analysis of the retirement benefit provision of the CPP indicated that without simplifying assumptions, one cannot generalize about the redistributive effects of the program. If one wants to consider the supplementary benefits and the implications of the plan for different cohorts, one must consider all of the possible variations in life histories. This can be done only by calculating the contributions and benefits for a representative sample of individuals. Since the plan is relatively new, the lifetime payments must be based on a simulation of the future life histories of the current population. This difficult task was done with the aid of a computer simulation system developed for this project. The simulation model is explained in detail in Appendix B.[9]

The model creates life histories for a sample of individuals that have the same age, sex, and provincial distribution in the base year (1966) as the actual census distribution. The 1972 Survey of Consumer Finances provided much of the information on labour force participation, earnings, income, unemployment, and duration of unemployment. As each sample individual ages, he faces certain probabilities of being in the labour force, being unemployed, etc. In the simulation system an individual's annual labour force participation, for instance, is randomly assigned on the basis of estimated probabilities. The result is a complete life history for as many individuals as desired. For this study a 1 in 2500 sample of the 1966 population was created. This sample consists of approximately 8000 individuals in 1966, but new individuals are added in subsequent years as birth and immigration augment the population.

For the purposes of analysing the distributional effects of the CPP the year-to-year fluctuations in an individual's earnings are particularly important. Because of a lack of information on these year-to-year movements a number of assumptions had to be made in the model. Year-to-year changes in the model occur where there are changes in variables such as labour force participation, unemployment, self-employment, education, age, or marital status. In addition the user of the model specifies a real rate of growth in earnings and other income that applies to all individuals.

Given life histories, the program calculates the CPP contributions and benefits for each person. The supplementary benefits such as disability benefits, orphans benefits, and spouses benefits are included. Every aspect of the plan from 1966 onward was built into the simulation program. For the years after 1974 it is assumed that the plan will remain unchanged. One feature of the early years of the plan was ignored. From 1966 onward it was assumed that spouses' benefits applied to men and women equally, as is now the case.

Since the CPP contributions and benefits are distributed over a lifetime, the present value of net benefits (present value of benefits minus present value of contributions) was calculated in the first year in which the contributor could

9 The model is based on an earlier model developed by Dobell and Cohen (1975).

potentially make contributions. This would be either 1966, the year in which he turned 18, or the year in which he entered Canada, whichever is later.[10] The present value calculation requires that one know a real rate of discount as well as a real rate of growth of earnings per worker and the rate of inflation. It was assumed that the real rate of growth of earnings per worker will be 2.5 per cent, the real rate of discount will be 2.5 per cent, and the rate of inflation will be 5 per cent. The average rate of growth in earnings per worker was 2.8 per cent between 1955 and 1974 (see chapter six). The assumed rate of discount compares directly with the real rate of return on Government of Canada bonds between 1958 and 1974 (see chap. 6, n. 5). Obviously a higher rate of discount will lower the value of the CPP. As noted previously, the rate of inflation has only a slight effect on the real present value of the CPP.

The simulation calculations indicate that when the plan was introduced in 1966 it 'created' wealth for the contributors in the sense that if the plan remained unchanged from 1974 on, it would give positive benefits to the contributors. This wealth creation occurs in a pay-as-you-go system whenever the rate of growth of earnings exceeds the discount rate and whenever a system is first established. No *real* wealth is created; wealth is simply transferred away from the 'terminal generation,' those who are denied benefits when the plan is eliminated. In 1966 the wealth created by the CPP and the QPP was equal to 37.2 billion dollars, net of taxes paid on benefits and taxes saved because of contributions. The implicit transfer of this amount of wealth was not done equally. For instance some age groups systematically benefited more than others. The simulation highlights the nature of these transfers.

Distribution between cohorts
The introduction of a pension plan that is financed partly on a pay-as-you-go basis is bound to redistribute wealth between cohorts or generations. As Browning (1973) points out, the pay-as-you-go method transfers income from the terminal generation, the generation that makes contributions and does not receive benefits, to the initial generation, the first generation to receive benefits. Similarly whenever contributions *and* benefits are increased, there is a transfer to those who contributed at the lower rate for at least part of their working lives. The opposite holds true for a decrease in contributions. This implies that it may be politically impossible to lower contributions and benefits in a pay-as-you-go system (Browning, 1973, 221). Those who have contributed at the higher rates will usually constitute a voting majority, and they will have an interest in perpetuating the system.

10 For purposes of benefit calculation the contribution period for immigrants includes years since age 18 (or 1966).

Table 11 shows the average present value of benefits minus employer and employee contributions under the CPP. These are expressed in 1966 prices. It should be realized that the table was generated from a sample of individuals and is therefore subject to a form of sampling error. This error accounts for some of the variation in present values in the table. The table indicates the general pattern of transfer that took place when the CPP was created. For the cohorts with contributions in 1966 it appears that the program was most generous for the 1925 to 1929 cohorts. The present value of the plan in 1966 was $5150 for this group. For those over age 18 in 1966 the present value tends to rise with age until age 37 to 41 and falls thereafter. It was indicated earlier in this chapter that without provision for years with low earnings and supplementary benefits those age 55 in 1966 appear to have the greatest net benefits. The simulation indicates that a period of contribution longer than ten years gives greater net benefits.

Net benefits increase for those born after the 1940s. There are several reasons for this result. First, the year's maximum pensionable earnings and year's basic exemption increase at a rapid rate after 1973. Second, net benefits are greater because of the higher earnings levels of the later cohorts.

Since benefits exceed contributions at a real rate of discount equal to 2.5 per cent, the plan is not actuarially sound at that real rate of interest. A higher rate of interest would lower the wealth transferred by the program, but much higher real rates are unrealistic. It is likely that the rates of contribution will be raised in order to cover rising expenditures. A rate increase will reduce the net benefits received by later cohorts.

Distribution between income classes – the CPP alone
The CPP undoubtedly produces some redistribution between income classes as well as between cohorts, but in a lifetime context it is somewhat difficult to define income. The measure chosen here is the present value of lifetime income converted to a lifetime annuity in constant dollars. This can be called permanent income. Two income measures were chosen, permanent income of the family (unmarried individual or husband and wife) and permanent earnings of the individual.

Tables 11, 12, 14, and 15 indicate that the net benefits tend to increase with both earnings and family income. This is true whether net benefits include taxation or not.[11] It does appear that the net benefits level off as earnings reach the higher levels. This occurs because of the limit on contributions and benefits

---

11 It should be noted that the high-income groups for the older cohorts are represented by a small sample.

TABLE 11

Average present value of benefits minus contributions (thousands of dollars)

Permanent earnings ($)	Cohort: 1895-9	1900-04	1905-9	1910-14	1915-9	1920-24	1925-9	1930-34	1935-9	1940-44	1945-9	1950-54	1955-9	1960-64
0-500	0.07	0.23	0.36	0.47	0.52	0.47	0.36	0.36	0.30	0.25	0.49	0.33	0.11	0.09
500-1000	0.43	1.78	3.25	3.27	4.22	3.53	2.45	2.48	1.67	1.53	1.50	1.41	0.75	0.44
1-2000	0.36	1.56	3.27	5.53	6.96	6.43	5.12	3.78	3.35	3.03	2.13	3.08	2.73	2.10
2-3000	0.48	1.67	3.76	8.75	8.74	7.31	6.97	7.06	4.92	5.39	4.01	4.50	4.56	3.80
3-4000	5.65	2.92	4.59	7.18	11.35	6.67	8.53	8.29	6.98	5.47	4.68	5.53	5.03	6.02
4-5000	0.0	1.39	4.11	7.71	7.80	11.27	8.67	9.03	8.36	5.25	7.00	5.43	7.02	7.23
5-6000	0.0	0.0	2.38	6.32	11.62	10.11	12.86	9.25	7.15	8.12	6.85	5.98	8.72	8.06
6-7000	0.0	-0.49	1.26	7.19	6.25	8.50	12.04	9.03	8.27	6.73	6.82	9.26	6.02	10.26
7-8000	0.0	0.0	-0.08	4.63	6.13	6.28	8.27	10.21	9.53	6.88	6.75	7.30	9.79	9.55
8-10,000	0.0	0.0	-0.31	5.52	9.84	11.61	9.50	8.25	7.05	6.80	6.69	7.57	9.93	13.97
10-12,000	0.0	0.0	-0.33	6.56	2.78	9.32	8.34	11.42	9.20	8.98	10.15	9.63	12.91	12.07
12-15,000	0.0	0.0	-0.06	3.92	2.47	8.40	7.79	7.46	9.77	7.90	8.80	7.87	12.19	14.28
15-20,000	0.0	0.0	0.0	7.02	8.00	4.51	7.53	7.87	7.27	9.69	8.40	11.25	14.07	17.77
20,000+	0.0	0.0	-0.56	0.0	11.45	7.43	9.09	11.13	4.91	9.10	7.41	13.57	14.82	20.72
Total	0.0	0.74	1.64	3.58	4.60	4.74	5.15	5.02	4.42	4.46	4.54	6.25	8.08	11.85

NOTE: 2.5 per cent real rate of interest, 5 per cent inflation, 2.5 per cent real rate of growth of earnings. Present values are in 1966 prices.

TABLE 12

Average present value of benefits minus contributions after taxes (thousands of dollars)

Permanent earnings ($)	Cohort: 1895-9	1900-04	1905-9	1910-14	1915-9	1920-24	1925-9	1920-34	1935-9	1940-44	1945-9	1950-54	1955-9	1960-64
0-500	0.06	0.22	0.36	0.45	0.49	0.46	0.35	0.34	0.28	0.24	0.46	0.32	0.11	0.09
500-1000	0.41	1.67	3.02	3.07	4.09	3.32	2.36	2.23	1.52	1.47	1.42	1.35	0.71	0.42
1-2000	0.29	1.52	3.21	5.15	6.10	5.82	4.81	3.41	3.02	2.79	1.90	2.86	2.46	1.85
2-3000	0.39	1.43	3.45	7.71	7.68	6.45	5.78	6.20	4.32	4.61	3.39	3.98	4.12	3.53
3-4000	4.40	2.66	4.15	6.23	10.23	5.52	7.41	7.35	5.72	4.62	3.94	4.85	3.94	5.72
4-5000	0.0	1.16	3.82	6.13	6.64	9.61	7.18	7.67	7.07	4.52	5.91	4.62	6.02	6.36
5-6000	0.0	0.0	2.00	5.39	10.29	8.82	11.21	7.83	6.39	6.62	5.75	4.88	7.69	6.06
6-7000	0.0	-0.27	1.50	6.36	5.57	7.61	10.50	6.98	7.79	5.84	5.05	8.20	4.74	8.79
7-8000	0.0	0.0	0.08	4.95	5.40	5.48	6.75	9.22	8.18	5.98	5.97	6.44	7.53	7.14
8-10,000	0.0	0.0	-0.20	4.90	7.99	9.64	8.68	7.09	6.20	6.29	5.51	6.38	7.98	11.08
10-12,000	0.0	0.0	-0.04	4.35	2.30	8.34	7.92	10.73	7.40	8.13	8.73	7.68	10.66	9.89
12-15,000	0.0	0.0	0.35	3.18	2.49	7.18	7.65	7.04	8.54	7.19	7.68	6.25	9.64	12.19
15-20,000	0.0	0.0	0.0	5.18	5.64	4.82	6.98	6.93	6.89	8.92	7.62	9.68	10.80	13.96
20,000+	0.0	0.0	-0.09	0.0	8.76	7.18	8.27	10.23	4.72	8.94	7.25	12.60	13.09	17.59
Total	0.0	0.70	1.54	3.17	4.07	4.18	4.57	4.44	3.86	3.99	3.97	5.47	6.82	9.93

NOTE: See note to Table 11

TABLE 13

Present value of benefits and contributions by cohort (thousands of dollars)

	Cohort: 1895-9	1900-04	1905-9	1910-14	1915-9	1920-24	1925-9	1930-34	1935-9	1940-44	1945-9	1950-54	1955-9	1960-64
Present value of benefits	0.0	0.87	1.89	4.07	5.30	5.69	6.52	6.68	6.38	6.97	7.48	10.43	13.94	20.53
Present value of contributions	0.0	0.13	0.25	0.49	0.70	0.95	1.37	1.66	1.96	2.51	2.94	4.18	5.86	8.68
Benefits minus contributions	0.0	0.74	1.64	3.58	4.60	4.74	5.15	5.02	4.42	4.46	4.54	6.25	8.08	11.85

NOTE: See note to Table 11.

TABLE 14

Average present value of benefits minus contributions (thousands of dollars)

Permanent income	Cohort: 1895-9	1900-04	1905-9	1910-14	1915-9	1920-24	1925-9	1930-34	1935-9	1940-44	1945-9	1950-54	1955-9	1960-64
0-500	0.06	0.22	0.20	0.12	0.0	0.14	0.0	0.0	0.0	0.0	0.0	0.0	-0.0	0.0
500-1000	0.11	0.37	0.76	0.49	1.42	0.92	0.75	0.24	0.01	0.38	0.01	-0.01	0.0	-0.00
1-2000	0.08	0.77	1.59	2.91	2.21	2.73	1.90	1.83	1.06	1.50	2.91	1.09	-0.02	0.23
2-3000	0.11	1.21	2.19	3.22	3.77	3.61	3.01	2.97	2.45	1.51	1.61	0.81	3.19	-0.02
3-4000	0.27	1.01	1.99	4.83	6.86	4.58	3.51	3.70	2.64	3.11	3.31	1.04	1.40	2.05
4-5000	1.05	1.11	2.49	4.16	6.08	5.49	4.70	4.96	4.84	3.29	2.76	3.10	5.33	5.54
5-6000	0.21	0.81	1.82	4.09	6.17	4.54	6.02	4.79	4.33	3.93	3.09	5.91	5.50	2.87
6-7000	0.41	2.16	2.18	6.29	4.45	4.83	7.40	4.65	5.91	4.26	3.62	4.28	2.61	5.39
7-8000	0.0	2.98	2.48	5.69	6.81	6.03	6.77	6.93	4.14	3.56	4.07	4.35	6.51	3.85
8-10,000	0.0	0.14	1.06	3.45	3.07	7.60	6.18	5.45	6.04	4.94	3.21	4.57	3.84	5.93
10-12,000	0.84	0.0	1.36	4.96	1.62	5.92	6.89	5.25	4.00	4.21	4.74	5.17	6.97	5.99
12-15,000	0.12	1.20	-0.00	3.63	4.17	3.22	6.54	7.16	5.44	5.65	6.89	5.00	6.71	7.08
15-20,000	0.33	0.33	3.34	8.86	6.18	3.67	6.09	4.54	4.40	6.29	5.05	7.08	7.76	8.95
20,000+	0.0	-0.58	2.25	4.78	7.17	9.58	6.49	7.15	4.92	5.90	6.72	9.28	10.47	14.40
Total	0.15	0.74	1.64	3.58	4.60	4.74	5.15	5.02	4.42	4.46	4.54	6.25	8.08	11.85

NOTE: See note to Table 11.

TABLE 15

Average present value of benefits minus contributions after taxes (thousands of dollars)

Permanent income	Cohort: 1895-9	1900-04	1905-9	1910-14	1915-9	1920-24	1925-9	1930-34	1935-9	1940-44	1945-9	1950-54	1955-9	1960-64
0-500	0.06	0.22	0.19	0.12	0.0	0.14	0.0	0.0	0.0	0.0	0.0	0.0	0.0	0.0
500-1000	0.11	0.37	0.75	0.49	1.42	0.92	0.76	0.24	0.01	0.38	0.01	-0.01	0.0	0.0
1-2000	0.08	0.76	1.57	2.88	2.17	2.70	1.91	1.80	1.05	1.47	2.91	1.11	-0.02	0.23
2-3000	0.10	1.18	2.15	3.04	3.50	3.42	2.90	2.90	2.28	1.46	1.58	0.83	3.14	0.0
3-4000	0.24	0.96	1.89	4.39	6.17	4.01	3.25	3.50	2.37	2.89	2.90	0.90	1.41	2.15
4-5000	0.83	0.98	2.44	3.75	5.44	4.80	4.24	4.56	4.36	2.96	2.57	2.86	5.27	5.32
5-6000	0.17	0.70	1.52	3.65	5.63	4.19	5.35	4.09	3.81	3.50	2.76	5.83	4.84	2.83
6-7000	0.34	1.85	1.99	5.24	3.86	4.14	6.59	4.09	5.39	3.65	3.07	3.75	2.26	5.04
7-8000	0.0	2.19	2.15	5.03	5.63	5.14	5.55	6.07	3.81	3.08	3.63	4.14	5.81	3.58
8-10,000	0.0	0.10	0.93	2.97	2.57	6.70	5.55	4.64	5.18	4.37	2.83	4.19	3.49	5.23
10-12,000	0.61	0.0	1.42	3.59	1.40	5.40	5.87	4.56	3.36	3.86	4.10	4.63	5.87	5.35
12-15,000	0.07	0.80	-0.01	2.71	3.78	2.98	6.03	6.21	4.68	5.07	5.75	4.20	6.05	6.49
15-20,000	0.29	0.23	2.01	5.89	4.42	3.05	5.14	3.91	3.94	5.28	4.63	6.13	6.43	7.46
20,000+	0.0	-0.26	1.34	2.71	5.07	6.46	5.20	6.18	3.86	5.46	5.77	7.93	8.66	11.94
Total	0.14	0.70	1.54	3.17	4.07	4.18	4.57	4.44	3.86	3.99	3.97	5.47	6.82	9.93

NOTE: See note to Table 11.

determined by the year's maximum pensionable earnings. The levelling off occurs at higher income levels for later cohorts because of the higher future values for YMPE.

These results are consistent with the theoretical conclusion discussed earlier in this chapter. If the CPP offers a net increase in wealth for the contributors, the increase will rise with income levels. At a higher rate of discount the net loss would also increase with income. The choice of the rate of discount is obviously extremely important. The 2.5 per cent rate was chosen because it approximates the real rate of return on Government of Canada bonds. A higher rate of discount does not seem reasonable because the CPP contributions are an even safer investment than a government bond. The benefits are free of risk resulting from unanticipated inflation.

Another problem related to the discount rate is that the rate of discount may vary systematically with income. Taxes should reduce the rate of return for higher-income groups, but those with higher incomes usually earn higher rates of return before taxes. Those with low incomes may have a higher rate of time preference and may be borrowers (at high rates of interest) rather than lenders. In effect the extent of forced saving is greater for those with lower incomes. They are forced to divert consumption to the future, while higher-income individuals are not forced to alter their consumption patterns. For purposes of examining the distributional effects it seems reasonable to use a uniform rate of discount, but it should not be forgotten that the forced saving will place a greater burden on the poor.

As an indication of the reasons for the regressive pattern of net benefits, Table 16 separates contributions and benefits for the 1945-9 cohorts. The table shows that contributions are more consistently related to total earnings than are the benefits. It follows that an increase in the contribution rate will make the program less regressive. Such an increase will make all contributors worse off when the CPP program is viewed by itself. The analysis of optimal financing indicated that an increase in the contribution rate would make the average person better off but would redistribute wealth between generations as well as between permanent income classes. In the second to last column of Table 16 the net benefits are calculated for a contribution rate that is double the current level. The net benefits are positive, but above the $4000 level they do not increase with earnings.

The net present value concept of redistribution tells us a completely different story from the internal rate of return. Since the benefit-contribution ratio falls as income increases, the internal rate of return will also be inversely related to income. The benefit-contribution pattern is captured if we calculate the contribution rate necessary to finance benefits with a 2.5 per cent rate of

TABLE 16

Present value of benefits and contributions, 1945-49 cohorts (thousands of dollars)

Permanent earnings (dollars)	PV of benefits	PV of contributions	Benefits minus contributions	Benefits minus 2 X contributions	Total contribution rate that equalizes benefits and contributions
0-500	0.54	.05	.49	.44	.389
500-1000	1.83	.33	1.50	1.17	.200
1-2000	2.91	.78	2.13	1.35	.134
2-3000	5.75	1.74	4.01	2.27	.119
3-4000	7.09	2.41	4.68	2.27	.106
4-5000	10.45	3.45	7.00	3.55	.109
5-6000	10.68	3.83	6.85	3.02	.100
6-7000	11.69	4.87	6.82	1.94	.086
7-8000	11.44	4.69	6.75	2.06	.087
8-10,000	11.91	5.22	6.69	1.47	.082
10-12,000	16.59	6.44	10.15	3.71	.093
12-15,000	14.95	6.15	8.80	2.65	.088
15-20,000	14.42	6.02	8.40	2.38	.086
20,000+	15.32	7.91	7.41	.50	.070
Total	7.48	2.94	4.54	1.60	.092

NOTE: See note to Table 11. The total contribution rate equals the sum of employer and employee contribution rates. The present total rate is 0.036.

discount.[12] The last column of Table 16 shows that this contribution rate (employer plus employee) falls with permanent earnings. For the reasons discussed above this measure is not an appropriate indicator of the redistribution effects of the CPP. This column tells us in effect that the CPP is progressive if the plan is actuarially sound. If it is not actuarially sound, it favours high income not low income contributors.

Other than the contribution rate and the pension rate (25 per cent), there are two key parameters of the CPP: the year's basic exemption (YBE) and the year's maximum pensionable earnings (YMPE). An increase in the YBE will make the plan less regressive if it is coupled with an increase in the contribution rate, but it will disqualify many low-income individuals from making contributions and from receiving the positive net benefits that the plan offers. An increase in the YMPE will increase the amount of net benefits of higher income contributors and

12 (Benefits/contributions) × .036 equals the rate that will equalize benefits and contributions.

will make the plan more regressive unless the contribution rate is increased sufficiently.

Distribution between income classes – the CPP
in the presence of other programs

The regressive nature of the CPP indicates that it rewards those with a relatively greater labour force commitment and higher earnings. However, there are other programs such as OAS, GIS, and GAINS that are designed to provide income for the aged. When the CPP is viewed together with these other programs, our conclusions are altered.

Consider the Guaranteed Income Supplement and GAINS. Both programs supplement the retirement income of those with little or no CPP benefits. These programs tax CPP benefits, at a 100 per cent rate in the case of GAINS. For an Ontario resident who expects to be eligible for GAINS the contributions to the CPP will result in no increase in retirement income. A single person in Ontario could receive a minimum income of $2890 from OAS, GIS, and GAINS in 1975 if he had no other income. The recipient without other income is taxed at a 100 per cent rate on the first $690 of CPP benefits and a 50 per cent rate on the remaining $854 of CPP benefits. Those with incomes from other sources will be taxed on their CPP benefits at the appropriate income tax rate which will be low because of the generous income tax provisions for those over 65 years of age.

In practice those with significant CPP benefits are likely to have income from other sources. The correlation of CPP benefits with other income means that a smaller amount of CPP benefits are subject to the 100 per cent tax. For instance, if private retirement income tends to be equal to CPP benefits, the first $345 of CPP benefits would be taxed at a 100 per cent rate and the next $427 at a 50 per cent rate. The remaining $772 would be taxed at the normal income tax rates, which depend on the type of income received.

The high tax rates on CPP benefits for those with little income of their own make the CPP program even more regressive, but this conclusion follows only if one accepts the notion that the CPP should be evaluated as if it were added to a world in which GIS and GAINS already existed. This point of view is not very relevant because historically GIS and GAINS were designed to supplement incomes for those with little income from the CPP or from private pensions. It makes more sense to consider the GIS and the GAINS programs as transfers to those with low lifetime earnings – i.e., low CPP benefits. These transfers are financed out of general revenues. To the extent that the tax system as a whole is progressive, GIS and GAINS result in a more equitable distribution of income. If we look at the GIS program as a transfer of wealth (just as the CPP is a transfer of

TABLE 17

Average net CPP benefits by marital status, sex, and cohort (thousands of dollars)

		Cohort: 1905-9	1910-14	1925-9	1935-9	1945-9	1955-9
Men	Ever-married	2.96	6.63	8.47	7.44	5.58	10.07
	Never-married	0.91	1.97	–	–	–	–
Women	Ever-married	0.48	0.84	1.68	1.41	1.94	3.89
	Never-married	0.97	2.07	–	–	–	–

NOTE: Excludes post-1966 immigrants. See also note to Table 11.

wealth), GIS is equivalent to a transfer of about $2000 at age 18 for those with no other retirement income.

Redistribution based on sex and marital status

The CPP offers more benefits to married than single contributors because of the surviving spouse's benefits and orphan's benefits. Since there are relatively few individuals who never marry during their lifetimes, the simulation contains few single individuals in the later cohorts. However, if we look at cohorts who entered the CPP at an older age, the differences in benefits can be seen. Consider as an example the 1910 to 1914 cohorts (Table 17). Men who have been married received over three times the benefits of the never-married men. This does not include the benefits that might be receivable because of the wife's contributions.

Table 17 also indicates the differences in benefits between men and women. The net benefits are somewhat larger for never-married women because of their greater longevity. The benefits for married women (excluding benefits based on the husbands' contributions) are much less than for married men because of their lower labour force participation and lower earnings. The relative gap appears to narrow for latter cohorts as women are much more likely to be contributors over a lifetime than over the last 10 or 20 years before retirement age.

There have been a number of proposals that housework be treated in the same way as employment in the market place. It is argued that married women should receive pension benefits for their employment in the household. In fact they do get such benefits, based on the husband's contributions, when the husband dies. (Widowers also receive such benefits.) The surviving spouse's benefits increase with the age of the survivor, implying a reward for past household services. These benefits are a direct transfer to married couples from single contributors. A problem arises when there is a divorce because no benefits are received for the years of household service. It has been suggested by the Conference of Welfare Ministers that the contribution credit be split between husband and wife in the event of a divorce or annulment (Canada, 1976). This proposal would increase the total benefits paid and would also increase the transfer away from never-married contributors. It may or may not result in an increase in GAINS or GIS payments.

Another proposal is that contributors who leave the labour force in order to raise children under the age of seven drop out those months of low (or zero) earnings from the calculation of average lifetime earnings (Canada, 1976). This is, in effect, an exemption of contributions for mothers with young children. It is a direct subsidy of child bearing, paid by those who do not have children. Considering the subsidies to those with children that already exist in the tax and transfer system and the subsidy of married contributors in the CPP system, this proposal cannot be justified on equity grounds. The proposal might also turn out to be highly regressive. It seems more reasonable to require that the husband make additional contributions on behalf of the wife's CPP account in order that single contributors do not subsidize married contributors. However, as long as the plan provides survivor's and orphan's benefits for married contributors, the single contributor (male or female) is relatively worse off than the married contributor.[13]

CONCLUSIONS

The introduction of the CPP implicitly transferred wealth between various economic groups. An analysis of the redistributional effects indicated that the CPP offers higher net benefits to those with higher permanent incomes. This conclusion would be altered if contribution rates were significantly increased or a higher rate of discount were used. If the plan were actuarially sound over-all, it would offer negative net benefits to those with higher earnings and positive net benefits to those with lower earnings.

The CPP also redistributes wealth from single individuals to married individuals because the rates of contribution are identical despite the additional benefits provided the married contributors. Greater net benefits go to married men than married women because of their higher earnings levels. Recent

13 If the plan offers negative net benefits, the additional contributions by the husband would make married couples worse off than before.

proposals that would integrate the housewife into the CPP system would redistribute wealth away from single contributors.

The gradual introduction of full benefits over a ten-year period provided greater net benefits for those contributing for a longer period of time. The 1925 to 1929 cohorts received the greatest wealth increase when the plan was introduced. Although the most recent cohorts receive an even larger net benefit because of their higher real earnings, future increases in the contribution rates will lower their net benefits.

If contributions are increased as suggested in chapter six, the CPP becomes less regressive, yet low income individuals will clearly bear an increased tax burden. This apparent contradiction can be explained if we realize that the alternative to a current increase in contribution rates is an even greater future increase. By increasing the burden on low income contributors today in order to fully fund the CPP, we will be relieving future low income contributors from the burden of supporting future pensioners. In order to achieve a fully-funded (progressive) system the tax burden must be increased on today's contributors.

In the discussion at the beginning of this chapter it was argued that the CPP should be considered as a contribution and benefit package. This package is generally regressive. When all the programs and tax provisions affecting the retirement population are taken into account, the system is probably slightly progressive at low-income levels, but the system would be more progressive without the CPP contributions on low earnings. A good argument can be made that society should force saving from those who might be so imprudent in their saving behaviour that they are burdens on society in their old age, but it is peculiar that taxes (contributions) are levied on those with incomes below the old age income support level and below the basic personal exemption level. A further problem is that these taxes lower the already small returns to work for the group that is likely to be discouraged from work by unemployment insurance and public assistance programs. The tax rates on low earnings may not be significant at today's rates of contributions, but the problem must be faced because contribution rates must invariably increase.

8
Incentive effects of
public retirement programs

Most transfer programs can be expected to influence the behaviour of the recipients. Usually, one is concerned about the response of labour supply to transfer programs. Retirement income programs are no exception, but they may have a more important effect on private saving and consumption over the recipient's lifetime. The potential effects of Canada's programs on labour supply and saving are analysed in this chapter.

LABOUR SUPPLY

The one period model
Before examining the effect of the programs on labour supply in a lifetime context, one must understand the single period implications during the retirement years. All of the programs increase the income for an individual in retirement. This increase in income will reduce both hours of work and labour force participation. The income will make retirement possible for some individuals who would not otherwise be able to retire.

Some of the programs not only increase the income of the recipient, they lower the marginal returns to work. Since OAS and the CPP do not decrease as other income increases, they do not lower the returns to work. The other programs induce substitution of leisure for income because of the implicit tax on earnings. GAINS taxes earnings at a 100 per cent rate which effectively eliminates incentives to work for those with low levels of earnings. As illustrated in Figure 1 those with more than $690 in income from the CPP or private sources will be subject to the 50 per cent tax rate associated with GIS. This implicit taxation will also serve to discourage work. The existence of the program may also encourage some pensioners to reduce their earnings in order to be eligible for GIS benefits. Ontario tax credit payments will induce substitution of leisure for income only for those with positive taxable income.

The income-tested programs (GIS, GAINS, and the OTC) will tend to have more powerful disincentive effects than OAS and the CPP, but all the programs will decrease work and labour force participation for those over age 65. This reduction in work causes a loss of real output in the economy. The tendency for work to decrease would be viewed more seriously if the programs affected younger workers. Canadian society views it as socially acceptable for those over age 65 to withdraw from the labour force. In fact one can argue that the objective of the programs is to facilitate this retirement. Furthermore, relatively few of those over 65 participated in the labour force before the introduction of CPP, GIS, and GAINS. Therefore, the disincentive effects on work are not of major concern.

The lifetime context

Consider someone who makes his lifetime labour supply and consumption decision at age 18 with certain knowledge of future wages, income from other sources, rates of interest, and retirement income programs. As long as he can borrow and lend at the same rate of interest, the income received in retirement from OAS, GIS, and GAINS will affect labour supply in all periods, as will the taxes paid to finance the programs. Work will tend to decrease and leisure will increase in response to the increase in wealth, assuming the benefits exceed the taxes paid during the working years (Rea, 1974a). This wealth effect is directly analogous to the income effect in a one period model.

The income-tested programs for a pensioner induce substitution of leisure for income after retirement. This substitution effect may induce a greater concentration of work during the pre-65 years for those who might be eligible for the income-tested programs. Others might be induced to increase their work after age 65 because of the lower income tax rates for pensioners. We can conclude that the substitution effects of the programs will induce more work after 65 for high-income individuals and less work after 65 for low-income individuals. When the wealth effect and the substitution effect are combined there may or may not be a net incentive to work for high-income individuals.

The CPP will have no effect on labour supply as long as the plan is actuarially sound (the present value of the future benefits equals the present value of the stream of contributions) and as long as CPP contributions are substituted for private saving (see below). If the present value of CPP benefits exceeds the

TABLE 18

Labour force participation rates, men and women over 65,
annual averages 1953-75

	Men	Women
1953	34.7	3.7
1954	33.2	3.8
1955	32.4	4.0
1956	34.0	4.5
1957	34.0	5.1
1958	32.1	5.3
1959	31.0	5.2
1960	30.3	5.6
1961	29.4	5.8
1962	28.5	5.6
1963	26.4	5.9
1964	26.8	6.3
1965	26.3	6.0
1966	26.3	5.9
1967	24.8	5.9
1968	24.4	6.0
1969	23.6	5.5
1970	22.7	5.1
1971	20.1	5.1
1972	18.8	4.4
1973	18.3	4.4
1974	17.9	4.2
1975	17.4	4.4

SOURCE: Statistics Canada, Cansim data base.

present value of the contributions, labour supply will be reduced in all periods
because of the wealth effect.

Recent trends

The life cycle labour supply effects predicted by economic theory cannot be
tested directly. However, the Canadian data are consistent with the hypothesis
that the programs have reduced the labour force participation rates of those over
age 65. Table 18 shows the trend in labour force participation for those over 65.
There has been a continued downward trend in the participation rates for men
during the period for which data are available. There appears to be an inverse
relationship between participation rate movements and the growth of public
retirement income programs. In regressions of participation rates for men and
women over 65 in the 1953 to 1975 period, the OAS plus GIS payment level

(adjusted for price changes) and the time trend were both statistically significant for men.[1] This was not the case for women. Unfortunately this statistical relationship does not prove causation. A reasonable alternative hypothesis is that the growth of public programs coincides with the growing need for these programs. The need is a result of the increasing prevalence of retirement at age 65.

PERSONAL SAVING AND CONSUMPTION

Theory
Economic models of the consumption-saving decision suggest that programs that provide retirement income will affect the individual's saving decision. If current income is ordinarily saved in order to provide retirement income, the availability of retirement income from a public program should reduce the amount of private saving. Whether or not this is true depends on the type of retirement program.

The Canada Pension Plan, unlike the Social Security system in the United States, does not tax earnings after age 65. This feature makes the analysis much less complicated. Figure 2 illustrates the consumption decision in a simple two period model with no labour supply adjustment. Personal saving falls by the amount of the contributions if the plan's return equals the market rate and if the desired saving exceeds the required contributions. If the plan offers a higher rate of return, the plan implicitly increases the consumer's wealth. Consumption will be likely to increase in all periods, and personal saving will fall by more than the amount of the contribution. Figure 3 illustrates this case in a two period model with no labour supply adjustment. Personal saving falls from B − E to C − D.[2] Those with no saving prior to the introduction of the pension would be forced to reduce their consumption because of the contributions. If possible they would choose to borrow against future pension benefits (move to segment HA) in order to increase current consumption.

The income-tested programs (GIS and GAINS) offer even more discouragement to individual saving. Those who expect to qualify for GAINS will have little incentive to save for their own retirement. Any returns to investment will be

---

1 Annual data for participation rates. The regressions were adjusted for autocorrelation using the Durbin method.
2 The pay-as-you-go in effect creates government debt in the form of promises to make pension payments in the future. If the plan is liquidated eventually and bequests are made between generations there may be no consumption and saving effects. See Barro (1974).

Figure 3

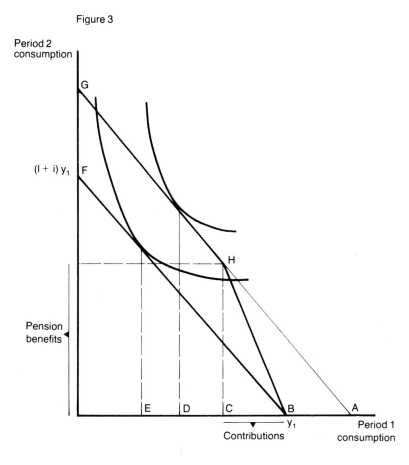

Period 2
consumption

G

$(l + i) y_1$ F

Pension
benefits

E   D   C   B   A

y_1

Contributions

Period 1
consumption

H

taxed at a 100 per cent rate. Funds accumulated in a Registered Retirement
Savings Plan would be subject to a 100 per cent tax on the principal as well as
the interest portion of the pension. Those qualifying for GIS benefits face a 50
per cent tax on the returns to an investment. By guaranteeing a minimum
income in retirement the government induces low-income workers to do little
saving of their own. However, it may be the case that those with low incomes are
simply unable to save regardless of the retirement income provisions.

The income tax provisions may encourage more saving on the part of
high-income individuals. The RRSP provisions allow one to defer income tax
until after age 65. The advantages are threefold: first, taxes are postponed,
second, investment income is accumulated tax-free, and third, marginal tax rates

will be lower after age 65 because of lower earnings and because of the pensioner tax exemptions. These provisions may encourage more saving than otherwise.[3]

Evidence

Empirical studies of the effect of pension programs on saving and consumption have produced mixed results. Feldstein (1974a) tests the hypothesis that the wealth created by US Social Security (AB in Figure 3) lowered personal saving in the US. He included social security wealth, the present value of future benefits minus contributions, in an aggregate consumption function. The coefficient of this variable was positive, implying an increase in consumption and a decrease in saving as a result of the social security system. Feldstein's results must be treated with scepticism (Upton, 1975). The size of the crucial coefficient and its significance are quite sensitive to the exact specification of the model. It is possible that this variable is merely a proxy for unknown variables that influence consumption.

Munnell (1974) did a similar study for the United States with results similar to Feldstein's. She also estimates the effect of pension income on saving for a sample of Consumers Union members. The results indicate that coverage by a pension plan or social security lowered savings for those aged 55 to 65. This contradicts Cagan's (1965) conclusion (based on the same survey) that persons eligible for pensions had higher rates of saving.[4]

There are difficulties in estimating the effect of pensions on savings which can explain the lack of hard evidence on this issue. First, those who have pensions may have a greater realization that they need to accumulate savings. Second, the receipt of pension income may be contingent on a reduction in labour supply after retirement age. The reduction in labour supply increases the desired saving during the pre-retirement years.

The simulation system described above generated the value of the wealth created in 1966 and subsequent years by the CPP and QPP. Since there are no wealth data for the Canadian household sector, the social security wealth had to be expressed as an increment to permanent income. In 1966 the net increase in permanent income was $1.6 billion as the result of the CPP and the QPP. The sum of the increase in permanent income and annual contributions produces a series that reflects the value of the CPP and QPP in terms of permanent income.[5] When

---

3 Some of the RRSP contributions may be borrowed rather than being financed out of current consumption.

4 Munnell refined the procedures used by Cagan.

5 This estimate assumes that contributions will remain constant in the future. It would be lower if the public expects contribution rates to increase.

entered into alternative consumption functions this variable consistently had a negative sign. This is not too surprising since the saving ratio has been relatively high since 1966. In short the data produced no evidence that the CPP and the QPP have affected saving in the manner described by Feldstein.

In summary the evidence on the private saving response to pensions does not offer strong support for the hypothesis that a program such as the CPP lowers private saving. One explanation for this lack of evidence is that many of those who pay contributions would not save in the absence of a pension. Those who are life cycle savers might reduce their saving only in response to a more generous program.

CONCLUSIONS

On balance the incentive effects of the existing structure of public pension programs are greatest for those with relatively low retirement incomes. Potential GAINS recipients will have no incentive to save for their retirement, and anyone who might otherwise work after age 65 for low annual earnings would be discouraged from working by the 100 per cent tax on private income.

These incentive effects must be put in perspective. The work disincentives are likely to be small when compared to the disincentives on younger workers produced by welfare programs because relatively few older people participate in the labour force. The saving reduction would be insignificant if those potentially affected would not save in the absence of public pension programs.

9
Summary and conclusions

The policies of the Province of Ontario regarding the role of private pension plans in the provision of retirement incomes are contained largely in the Pension Benefits Act of 1965. The Act seeks to protect members of private pension plans in three distinct ways: (1) to minimize the loss of pension rights when employees change jobs by explicitly setting forth regulations concerning the vesting and portability of pension benefits; (2) to ensure that the private pension plans are financially solvent; and (3) to ensure that employers provide adequate information to employees regarding the details of the plan. The Pension Benefit Act specifies a minimum vesting requirement of the attainment of age 45 *and* the completion of ten years of service, after which the employee becomes entitled to a deferred pension equal to his earned pension under the plan. Benefits which vest are 'locked-in' since the employee is *not* allowed to withdraw either his contributions or the contributions paid on his behalf. The Act thus seeks to ensure that the vested benefits are taken in the form of a deferred pension rather than in the form of a cash withdrawal.

The analysis in chapter two indicated that pension benefits, to the extent that they reflect employer contributions, are a form of deferred wages. These deferred wages, in turn, are a part of the total compensation package with which employers compete for workers in competitive labour markets. In order to protect an employee from the loss of these deferred wages when he changes jobs, one can argue that vesting ought to be full and immediate. In advocating a change in this direction, the present authors recognize that the elimination of delayed vesting is likely to produce effective wage grids which more sharply reward years of service. To the extent that compensatory changes in effective wage grids do occur, turnover will continue to impose costs on the terminating employee, although these costs will be less discontinuous than those implied by delayed vesting regulations.

The argument that vesting ought to be full and immediate requires an additional qualification. With the exception of money purchase and non-contributory defined benefit plans, the employee may pay most of the cost of his accrued pension benefits during his early working years. As a result, liberalization of vesting provisions to permit benefits to vest at an earlier age than (say) 40 may be largely illusory since the employers' contributions to which the employee becomes entitled (i.e., the actuarial value of the deferred pension less the accumulated value of the employee's own contributions) are likely to be minimal. The popularity of the goal of relaxing vesting requirements suggests that it is not well known that the young employee in a contributory defined benefit plan may directly pay virtually all of the cost of the deferred pension to which he becomes entitled.

The current 'locking-in' provisions, with their severe restrictions on individual discretion, can be justified only by the existence of costs imposed on society as a whole (in the form of a higher actuarial claim on income-related supplementary pension programs of both the federal and Ontario governments) if an individual does not adequately provide for his own retirement income. This externality argument, however, is weakened by the presence of the Canada Pension Plan. The existence of this plan, in which the worker's benefits vest immediately and are completely 'locked-in,' reduces – but does not eliminate – the probability that a terminating employee who opts for cash withdrawal will ultimately draw benefits from an income-related public pension program.

A comparison with a Registered Retirement Savings Plan (RRSP) illustrates an inequity contained in the 'locking-in' of employer and employee contributions. Consider the case of an employee who receives his *full* wages currently, including the actuarial equivalent of the employer contribution which would otherwise be made on his behalf to the pension plan, and saves for his retirement in the form of an RRSP. The contributions to the RRSP are 'locked-in' only to the extent that tax incentives discourage the liquidation of the RRSP prior to the employee's retirement. Statutory 'locking-in' provisions thus limit the financial options of the member of the employer-sponsored pension plan relative to those of the individual who saves for his retirement in the form of a RRSP.

Significantly, Ontario's Pension Benefits Act of 1965 contains no explicit provisions to protect members of private pension plans from the problems which might arise in an inflationary climate. The problems posed by inflation for the private pension system constitute the subject matter of chapters three and four. One can argue persuasively that the viability of private pension plans hinges upon their ability to provide adequate retirement incomes in an inflationary climate. The provision and preservation of an employee's pension benefits in an inflationary climate can be treated in two stages: (1) the preservation of the real value of pension benefits as they accumulate during the employee's work years, and (2) the preservation of the real value of these benefits during his retirement years. The analysis contained in these chapters indicates that final earnings plans are the most successful of the popular pension plans in ensuring the adequacy of pension benefits as they accumulate during an employee's work years, and that the full indexation of pension benefits during the employee's retirement years is required if the real value of the pension benefits is not to be eroded by inflation which occurs after the employee has begun to draw his pension.

Problems posed by inflation for final earnings plans, including the possible rise in experience deficiencies, are treated at length in the chapter three. The analysis indicates that final earnings plans can remain actuarially sound in an inflationary climate (i.e., they will not suffer large increases in experience deficiencies) so long as the real returns on the assets which comprise their investment portfolios are unaffected by inflation. This issue, in turn, invites an empirical study of the impact of inflation on the real returns of both fixed-income securities and common stocks. The conclusions of this study, reported at length in Appendix A, suggest that the real returns on a portfolio consisting of fixed-income securities and/or common stocks is likely to fall in a period of accelerating inflation. This result serves to explain the sharp rise in the experience deficiences of final earning plans during the recent period of accelerating inflation in Canada. The analysis also suggests that the amortization period for experience deficiences be extended, a result which may help to encourage employers to establish final earnings plans.

The fundamental question addressed in chapter four is whether a private pension plan can remain actuarially sound and yet provide full indexation of pension benefits during an employee's retirement years. Analysis indicates that the answer is yes so long as the real return on the assets which comprise the investment portfolios of private pension plans are unaffected by inflation. As noted previously, the study summarized in Appendix A indicates that the real returns on a portfolio consisting of fixed-income securities and or common stocks is *not* likely to be neutral with respect to inflation. The implication is that private pension plans, given their eligible set of investment opportunities, cannot provide indexed benefits after retirement and remain actuarially sound.[1] The

---

1 The importance in costing pension plans of the assumed relationship between the nominal return on investment and the rate of inflation again merits emphasis. As noted, if the nominal return rises in tandem with inflation, then a pension plan which is actuarially sound in a non-inflationary climate will remain actuarially sound in an inflationary one. In his analysis of the costs of indexing pensions, Calvert (1977, 85-91)

analysis thus indicates that private pension plans *could* provide adequate retirement incomes in an inflationary climate if their funds could be invested in index bonds or their equivalent. One cannot recommend that the government respond to this need by providing an index bond, however, in the absence of a comprehensive study of the impact on the Canadian financial system of the introduction of such a financial instrument. Realistically, one can argue that the likelihood of the government's providing an index bond or its equivalent would increase if its impact on the Canadian financial system could be minimized.

One alternative to the outright provision of index bonds, for example, would be for the government to underwrite the sale of indexed annuities. The annuities would provide a fixed *real* interest rate and would be sold only to the employee (or the guarantor of his plan) at the time of his retirement. Private pension plans – especially those of the final earnings variety – could be designed to provide the necessary capital sum at the time of the employee's retirement to purchase the appropriate annuity. In principle, life insurance companies in the private sector could also sell indexed annuities, although their ability to assume this inflation risk is limited by the conventional set of investment opportunities available to them. At the same time, the sale of indexed annuities by the government would place, via competitive forces, great pressure on life insurance companies to offer indexed annuities as well. This pressure, in turn, would greatly increase the demand *by* life insurance companies for index bonds or their equivalent, which might ultimately – as in the case of the outright provision by the government of index bonds – lead to a major transformation of the Canadian financial system. In short, any government attempt to provide a means whereby private pension plans are able to offer indexed benefits after retirement will run the risk of producing a major change in the structure of the Canadian capital market. Although such a change may ultimately prove to be desirable, its potential magnitude forces one to proceed with caution in recommending that the government provide an index bond or its equivalent.

PUBLIC PENSION PROGRAMS

Since private pensions do not cover large segments of the population and since their benefits are not fully indexed with respect to inflation, there is a need for

makes the implicit assumption that the *nominal* return is constant regardless of the rate of inflation. Not surprisingly, his results then indicate that the costs of indexation are quite enormous. The evidence presented in this text only indicates that the nominal return on a typical pension fund is not likely to rise sufficiently to match an increase in the rate of inflation. The data suggest, especially since the majority of pension funds are still invested in fixed-income securities, that the *nominal* return should nonetheless rise with inflation.

public programs for the aged. Programs such as the Guaranteed Income Supplement and Guaranteed Annual Income System provide support for low income individuals over 65, while the Old Age Security program provides income to all individuals over 65. The Canada Pension Plan in effect forces those in the labour force to save for their own retirement. Each of these programs attempts to fulfil one or more of the objectives of public policy: (1) to provide an income for the aged with minimal alternative means of support; (2) to pass on some of the current increases in real income to older members of society; (3) to provide for means by which individuals (or their employers) can save for their own retirement income; and (4) to ensure that the public or private plans do not overly distort the individual's incentives to work and save.

A variety of issues are inevitably raised in any discussion of the financing of the CPP. These include, for example, the impact of alternative financing arrangements on private savings and investment, the implications for the intergenerational distribution of wealth, the safety of the pensions promised by the program, and the implications of an increase in the retired population. At an abstract level, one can demonstrate that the choice between pay-as-you-go and fully-funded pension systems depends on the relationship between the social rate of return on capital and the rate of growth of earnings. Since empirical evidence suggests that the former exceeds the latter, an investment fund is desirable for Canada. In practice, the CPP fund purchases provincial debt rather than making direct investment in the private sector. A purchase of provincial debt leads to real investment (or no decrease in real investment) if the provinces do not increase their current expenditure in response to the readily available CPP funds. A move towards a larger CPP fund, as appears to be optimal, must be accompanied by a greater realization by the provinces that their obligations to the CPP fund are real. An increase in the interest rate paid to the CPP fund might help deter additional provincial expenditures, but a preferred route might be to have the CPP fund purchase securities from the private sector.

The future population growth has important implications for the financing of public pension plans. A lower rate of growth of population will increase the pensioner ratio, which in turn increases the contribution rate required to finance a pay-as-you-go system. One can expect the pensioner ratio and the contribution rate under a pay-as-you-go system to approximately double in the next 50 years. The contribution rates under an investment fund (once established) will not be affected by the changing age structure of the population. Regardless of the financing method the CPP contribution rate will have to be increased. The decision to be made is how much and how soon contribution rates should be increased.

A lowered retirement age would require increased pay-as-you-go contribution rates in order for the reduced working population to support the increased retired population. The Canadian Labour Congress has suggested that the retirement age be lowered to 60. In 1971 the lowering of the retirement age to 60 would have increased the pensioner ratio by 53 per cent, requiring a 53 per cent increase in the long run pay-as-you-go contribution rate. If 60- to 64-year-old workers retire, employment and national income will be lowered. Each individual's lifetime earnings will fall because of the reduction in lifetime work. It is not unreasonable for workers to wish to retire earlier, provided they are aware that they must give up some income in exchange for the added leisure. With a pay-as-you-go pension system, those who are 60 when the retirement age is lowered from 65 to 60 will naturally gain the most, but in the long run contribution rates must increase and consumption must decrease during the working years in order to finance an increased period of retirement.

Some observers have argued that public pension programs induce individuals to lower their private saving for retirement. On the whole, the evidence on this issue is somewhat contradictory. For Canada, there is no evidence at the aggregate level that the introduction of the CPP and QPP has reduced private saving. The impact of public retirement programs on the incentive to work is also of concern. The income-tested retirement programs tax earnings and encourage substitution of leisure for income. The increased availability of retirement income also produces a wealth effect that should lower work. The secular decline of labour force participation rates for older men is consistent with this hypothesis, but the growth of retirement programs may be the *result* of this decline in participation.

The redistribution inherent in a transfer program that provides negative benefits in one period and positive benefits in another is subject to some controversy. The theoretical analysis in chapter eight indicated that one should consider jointly the redistribution impact of the CPP contributions and benefits. The analysis also indicated that the appropriate concept for redistribution analysis is the amount of wealth transferred, not the rate of return inherent in the program. A regressive program was (arbitrarily) defined as one which transfers a greater amount of wealth to those with higher permanent incomes. One can show that the basic retirement benefit provisions in the CPP are regressive if the plan is not actuarially sound, as is now the case. If contributions are increased so that the plan is actuarially sound on average, the plan will be progressive. Those with low permanent incomes will receive positive net benefits and those with higher permanent incomes will receive negative net benefits.

The conclusion described above was supported when the entire system was simulated with a life cycle model of the Canadian population. The net benefits were greatest for those with relatively high incomes. The CPP was also found to redistribute wealth from single individuals to married individuals because the rates of contribution are identical despite the additional benefits provided the married contributors. Greater net benefits go to married men than to married women because of their higher earnings levels. Recent proposals that would integrate the housewife into the CPP system would redistribute wealth away from single individuals.

The gradual introduction of full benefits over a ten-year period provided greater net benefits for those contributing for a longer period of time. The 1925 to 1939 cohorts received the greatest wealth increase when the plan was introduced. Although the most recent cohorts receive an even larger net benefit because of their higher real earnings, future increases in the contribution rates should lower their net benefits.

Analysis indicates that the CPP itself is regressive at low levels of permanent income, but when other programs are taken into account, the system is probably progressive at low income levels. Nevertheless, the CPP requires contributions from those with levels of income below the basic personal exemption level in the income tax act; in other words, those considered poor. Since overall contribution rates must be raised in the future, regardless of whether or not an investment fund is created, the tax system will become more regressive unless modifications are made in the contribution formula.

There are two strategies open for the CPP system if it is to avoid the regressive features and forced saving on the part of those with very low incomes. The first strategy is to run the CPP as a pension program for those with moderate incomes. The YBE could be raised to eliminate the contributions on low earnings, and the contribution rates could simultaneously be increased. The GIS and GAINS programs would provide income for those with low CPP benefits. The disadvantage of this approach is that low-income individuals would not be entitled to disability benefits and other provisions of the CPP.

The second alternative is for the general revenue fund to make contributions on behalf of those with low income. This might be accomplished by adding an additional exemption above the YBE. Low income workers would in effect be subsidized in the form of accumulated entitlement to CPP benefits. This subsidy would offer an encouragement to work for workers with low earnings.[2] (Of course tax rates would be higher for those with higher income.) The advantage of this approach is that the contributory system is maintained. The same general approach could also be used to generate CPP entitlement for housewives in low income families. It is our view that contributions for a housewife in a higher income family should be made out of that family's income, not out of the income of single men and women.

2 In a static context the program would have incentive and disincentive effects similar to those for an earnings subsidy (Rea, 1974b).

A third strategy would be to eliminate the CPP as it now exists and operate a general income maintenance system for those over 65. This alternative can be rejected on at least two grounds. First, it has been shown that it is desirable to create an investment fund in order to finance old age pensions. A general income maintenance program would be unlikely to lead to such a fund. Second, there is a need for a government-guaranteed pension system for middle income groups. The government is able to offer pensions that are free of the risk of unanticipated inflation, while the private sector has difficulty in eliminating this risk. A mix of public and private programs provides a portfolio balance for the large portion of society.

The public programs have three major components, a lump sum transfer to all those over 65, tax reductions for higher income groups, and guaranteed income programs for lower income groups. The contributory program, the CPP, does not provide very significant benefits when compared to all of the other programs. One could argue that the tax provisions are a way of compensating for the effect of inflation on those living on private pensions. However, it seems more reasonable for the government to take a more direct role in facilitating private saving for retirement. This might be accomplished with three modifications of the present system: first, an expansion of the CPP benefits and contributions; second, improved regulations governing private pension plans (described above); and third, provision of a financial instrument, such as a life-time annuity at age 65, that protects the individual's private pension from erosion by inflation. These three steps would allow the majority of Canadians to provide for their own retirement and eliminate some of the justification for Old Age Security and tax advantages for high income pensioners.

Inflation and the rates of return on bonds and equities: some Canadian evidence

INTRODUCTION

The ultimate criterion for assessing the viability of private pension plans must be their ability to provide adequate retirement incomes for their participants. Final earnings plans (or re-negotiated flat benefit plans) are likely to preserve the real value of pension benefits as they accumulate during an employee's work years, while indexation of pension benefits during an employee's retirement years is necessary to preserve their real value in an inflationary climate. The recent escalation in the rate of inflation in Canada, however, has produced huge increases in the experience deficiencies of final earnings plans, increases which must either be financed out of operating earnings or recaptured from plan members in the form of higher contribution rates. Both options, of course, have important implications for the redistribution of income. Further, few private pension plans provide for the indexation of benefits upon retirement, with the result that the recent surge in inflation has seriously eroded the real value of pension benefits which are currently being disbursed.

In short, recent experience casts doubt on the ability of private pension plans, at least in their current form, to provide adequate retirement incomes in an inflationary climate. Recent experience also invites additional questions. To what extent, for example, will final earnings plans suffer from increased experience deficiencies in periods of (1) high inflation or (2) escalating inflation? Can private pension plans index pension benefits during an employee's retirement years and remain actuarially sound? The answers to these questions depend in large part on the extent to which the yields on the assets in pension plans' portfolios respond to inflation. If, for example, the real returns on these assets were unaffected by inflation, whether expected or unexpected, then pension plans could fully *anticipate* inflation. This result, in turn, would ensure that plans of the final earnings variety (for example) would not suffer from higher experience deficiencies in an inflationary climate, and would also enable private pension plans to index pension benefits during an employee's retirement years and yet remain actuarially sound.

The rapid increase in the experience deficiencies of private pensions plans during the current inflationary climate suggests, of course, that these plans cannot fully anticipate inflation. In part, this problem can be traced to the presence of bonds acquired at various points in time, and whose coupons in nominal terms are thereby fixed for various periods into the future, in the portfolios of most private pension plans. The presense of these bonds, in effect, renders it impossible for most plans to anticipate inflation even if (1) that inflation is expected, and (2) nominal interest rates adjust upward by the exact amount of any increase in expected inflation. In addition, any increase in inflation which is unexpected serves to reduce the real return on all bonds which have been acquired previously.

The goal of the empirical research summarized in this appendix is thus to determine the impact of both expected and unexpected inflation on the rates of return on bonds and equities. The evidence so obtained, in turn, should provide some perspective on the more important question of the extent to which inflation can be anticipated. The appendix is divided into two parts: the first analyses the impact of price expectations and the degree of uncertainty with which these price expectations are held on the nominal yields of bonds of varying maturities; the second analyses the impact of both expected and unexpected inflation on the realized rates of return on equities for a variety of different holding-periods.

In general, the impact of inflation on the rates of return on bonds and equities is central to an understanding of the operation of private pension plans in an inflationary climate. Although bonds, for the reasons cited above, limit the ability of pension plans to anticipate inflation, equities may provide a vehicle for doing so. Further, the extent to which nominal interest rates adjust to price expectations, and perhaps also to uncertainty with regard to the future course of inflation, should provide an important perspective on the ability of private pension plans to anticipate inflation.

I INFLATION AND THE RATE OF RETURN ON BONDS

The empirical analysis explores two avenues through which inflation affects the nominal – and ultimately the real – rate of return on bonds: (1) the extent to which price expectations are incorporated into nominal interest rates, and (2) the extent to which the degree of uncertainty with which price expectations are held influences these nominal returns. Following Irving Fisher (1970), economists have long argued that an increase in the expected rate of inflation will lead nominal interest rates, for the same time horizon, to adjust upward by an identical amount. If both borrowers and lenders expect inflation to increase by one per cent, for example, competitive forces will ensure that nominal interest rates rise by one per cent as well. More recently, Darby (1975) has argued that nominal interests should rise by *more* than the increase in the expected rate of inflation if the real *after-tax* return to lenders is to be unaffected. Finally, economic theorists have argued (see, for example, Hicks, 1946) that increased uncertainty regarding future movements in interest rates, which reflects in large part uncertainty regarding the future course of inflation, should raise long-term relative to short-term interest rates and perhaps the general level of interest rates as well. In short, economic theory identifies two channels through which inflation can affect the nominal yields on bonds.

The attempt to obtain empirical evidence on these issues requires two key inputs: (1) a model of the determinants of nominal interest rates which is suitable for the analysis of the impact of price expectations, and (2) a procedure for approximating the unobserved market forecasts of inflation. In order to ensure that the results are not unique to any specific model of interest rate determination or to any specific proxy for inflationary expectations, one would like to examine these issues in the context of several alternative models and for two or more different procedures for measuring inflationary expectations.

Recently, Carr and Smith (1972), Jenkins and Lim (1973), Yohe and Karnosky (1969), and Feldstein and Eckstein (1970) have proposed and tested alternative models of the determinants of nominal interest rates. The unifying theme in the construction of these alternative models has been the desire to focus explicitly on the role of price expectations, and these four models thus represent candidates in which to explore the issues identified at the beginning of this section. Earlier work by Pesando (1976) indicated, however, that the Feldstein-Eckstein model performed quite poorly with Canadian data, a result foreshadowed by certain theoretical limitations of the model. Only the Yohe-Karnosky, Carr-Smith, and Jenkins-Lim models are thus employed as alternative frameworks in which to assess the impact of (1) inflationary expectations and (2) inflation risk (i.e., the degree of uncertainty with which price expectations are held) on nominal interest rates of bonds with varying maturities. Inflationary expectations, in turn, will be proxied in two distinct ways: (1) by invoking the rational expectations hypothesis (Pesando, 1976; and Carr, Pesando, and Smith, 1976) to create synthetic price expectation series, and (2) by the standard procedure of employing distributed lag proxies for price expectations. The alternative models and the different procedures for approximating the (non-observable) market forecasts of inflation are discussed in turn.

The alternative models of the determinants of nominal interest rates
As noted previously, three models of the determinants of nominal interest rates are employed as alternative frameworks in which to investigate the impact of price expectations on nominal interest rates. These three models are sketched briefly below.

1 The Yohe-Karnosky model
The Yohe and Karnosky (Y-K) model seeks to explain fluctuations in nominal interest rates (r) solely in terms of the Fisher effect, i.e. in terms of variations in price expectations (P^*). The model presumes that the variations in nominal interest rates are primarily due to variations in price expectations and that the variety of forces which may shock real interest rates are orthogonal to their distributed lag proxies for inflationary expectations. After adding a disturbance term (u_t), one can write the Y-K model as follows:

$$r_t = a_0 + a_1 P_t^* + u_t. \tag{A1}$$

2 The Carr-Smith model
The Carr and Smith (C-S) model attempts to synthesize two monetary channels which affect interest rates. In the spirit of Wicksell, C-S construct a variable to measure the difference between the actual ($\dot{M}_t$) and expected ($\dot{M}_{t-1}^*$) rate of growth of the money supply. An increase (decrease) in the unanticipated rate of growth of the money supply is hypothesized to lower (raise) interest rates. In the spirit of Fisher, C-S assume that changes in the money supply affect the actual and ultimately the expected rate of inflation, and hence introduce a price expectations variable to explain the nominal rate of interest.

The C-S model can be written as follows:

$$r_t = a_0 + a_1 P_t^* + a_2 (\dot{M}_t - \dot{M}_{t-1}^*) + u_t. \tag{A2}$$

3 The Jenkins-Lim model
The Jenkins and Lim (J-L) model reflects the belief that the real interest rate evolves slowly over time and that the variance of the nominal rate primarily reflects the variance of price expectations. The real interest rate can be shocked by both monetary policy (as reflected in the rate of acceleration of the money supply) and variations in the rate of growth of the real government debt ($\dot{g}$) held by the general public. The J-L model may be written as follows:

$$r_t = a_0 + a_1 P_t^* + \sum_{i=0}^{k} a_{2i} (m_{t-i} - m_{t-i-1}) + \sum_{i=0}^{n} a_{3i} \dot{g}_{t-1} + u_t. \tag{A3}$$

Note that these three theories all highlight the importance of price expectations as a determinant of nominal interest rates. Indeed the Y-K model presumes that the variance of nominal interest rates is due almost exclusively to the variance in inflationary expectations. The C-S and J-L models proceed one step further by attempting to isolate forces which influence real interest rates as well. Both the C-S and J-L models possess the desirable property that a steady long-term (and hence expected) rate of growth of the money supply will not directly affect nominal interest rates, but will influence them only indirectly via its impact on the actual and hence the expected rate of inflation.

The alternative measures of price expectations
As noted previously, two alternative procedures are employed to approximate the price expectations that prevail in the market: (1) the standard distributed lag proxies, and (2) synthetic price expectations series constructed by invoking the rational expectations hypotheses. These two procedures are discussed briefly below.

1 Distributed lag proxies for price expectations
In their respective studies, Y-K, C-S, and J-L all employ standard distributed lag proxies for inflationary expectations. This procedure involves the assumptions that individuals employ (only) information contained in the past history of inflation when formulating their forecasts of future inflation and that the use of this information is adequately captured in a fixed weight distributed lag relationship. The forecast of inflation made in period t for period $t+1$ ($_{t+1}\dot{P}_t^*$) is thus presumed to bear the following relationship to the observed history of inflation:

$$_{t+1}\dot{P}_t^* = \sum_{i=0}^{n} \beta_i \dot{P}_{t-i}. \tag{A4}$$

For simplicity, let $f(z)$ denote the forces which are presumed to impinge on the real rate of interest in the Y-K, C-S, and J-L models. One can then write the common framework employed to investigate the impact of price expectations on nominal interest rates of one-period maturity as follows:

$$r_t = f(z) + a* \sum_{i=0}^{n} \beta_i \dot{P}_{t-i} \tag{A5}$$

$$= f(z) + \sum_{i=0}^{n} w_i \dot{P}_{t-i}, \text{ with } w_i = a\beta_i. \tag{A5'}$$

In equation (A5), the coefficient a designates the extent to which price expectations are incorporated into the nominal interest rate. Estimation of the several models, however, will produce the results indicated in equation (A5'), in which a and β_i's are both contained in the estimated parameters (the w_i's). In effect, the structural parameters are not identified. The standard solution to this problem, employed either explicitly or implicitly in the literature, is to impose the identifying restriction that the $\sum_{i=0}^{n} \beta_i$ is equal to unity. This procedure enables one to equate the sum of the estimated distributed lag coefficients with the key (unobserved) parameter a :

$$\sum_{i=0}^{n} w_i = \sum_{i=0}^{n} a\beta_i = a \sum_{i=0}^{n} \beta_i = a. \qquad (A6)$$

The logic of imposing this identifying restriction is that it implies that a sustained increase of one per cent in the actual rate of inflation will ultimately cause individuals to revise upward their forecasts of future inflation by one per cent as well. Nonetheless, this identifying restriction has been the subject of considerable criticism (Sargent, 1971). The importance of the identifying restriction cannot be overstated. If, for example, individuals take into account the trend in past price behaviour in formulating price expectations so that the sum of the lagged weights is greater than one, say 1.10, then coefficient of 1.0 for $\sum_i w_i = a \sum \beta_i$ obtained in the nominal interest rate equation (equation 5') would indicate that nominal interest rates adjust .909 basis points for every 1.0 per cent change in the expected rate of inflation. Since the sum of the lagged weights and price expectations are jointly determined, the identifying assumption is required and conclusions drawn from the distributed lag approach hinge on the assumption that $\sum \beta_i = 1$.

2 Synthetic price expectations and the rational expectations hypothesis

In addition to the problems associated with the identifying restrictions noted above, distributed lag proxies for price expectations have at least two other important limitations. First, their use in empirical studies is equivalent to assuming that investors employ only information contained in the observed history of inflation in formulating their forecasts of future inflation. This assumption has been challenged, for example, by Kane and Malkiel (1976), Modigliani and Shiller (1972) and Rutledge (1974a). Second, researchers who employ distributed lag proxies for price expectations generally have devoted little attention to the issue of whether or not the forecasting mechanisms implicit in their lag estimates are consistent with rational forecasting behaviour. Gibson (1972) and Pyle (1972) attempted to circumvent these problems by incorporating the price expectations data compiled by Joseph A. Livingston, the financial columnist, into their empirical tests of alternate models of the determinants of nominal interest rates. The resulting evidence, obtained from US data, is tainted in view of the demonstration by Pesando (1975c) that the Livingston price expectations are not rational. This fact serves to cast doubt on the assumption, implicit in their use in empirical studies, that the Livingston price expectations are representative of those of market participants generally.

The second approach to attempt to circumvent the problems associated with the non-observability of market forcasts of inflation is thus to invoke the rational expectations hypothesis of John F. Muth (1961) to create synthetic price expectations series. As initially defined by Muth, rationality requires that expectations be generated by a reduced-form equation in the exogenous variables which actually generate the variable to be predicted. Empirical researchers, however, have employed a modified (and weaker) form of Muth's hypothesis. (See, for example, Modigliani and Shiller, 1973; Sargent, 1972; Pesando, 1975a, 1975b, 1975c). Expectations are defined as rational if they fully incorporate all the relevant information that is available at the time the forecast is made. In order to make this concept operational, one must define the specific information set upon which expectations are assumed to draw. For the purpose of this paper, the information set from which investors are presumed to form their forecasts of future rates of inflation is assumed to consist of the observed histories of both the nominal interest rate and the rate of inflation. This information set together with the rational expectations hypothesis permits one to construct a synthetic series of price expectations over alternative time horizons as follows.

Assume that forecasts of the real interest rate and the rate of inflation are based — directly or indirectly — on the information contained in the histories of these two variables. The forecasts made in period t of the real interest rate $(_{t+1}i_t^*)$ and the rate of inflation $(_{t+1}P_t^*)$ expected to prevail in period $t+1$ may be written as follows:

$$_{t+1}i_t^* = \sum_{j=1}^{n} a_j^{(1)} i_{t-j+1} + \sum_{j=1}^{n} \beta_j^{(1)} P_{t-j+1} ; \tag{A7}$$

$$_{t+1}P_t^* = \sum_{j=1}^{n} c_j^{(1)} i_{t-j+1} + \sum_{j=1}^{n} d_j^{(1)} P_{t-j+1} . \tag{A8}$$

Since the real interest rate is defined *ex post* as the nominal interest rate less the realized rate of inflation, the information contained in the variables on the right-hand-side of equations (A7) and (A8) may be viewed (equivalently) as consisting of the information contained in the histories of the nominal interest rate and the rate of inflation.

According to the rational expectations hypothesis, the parameters of (A7) and (A8) should be estimated using equations (A9) and (A10):

$$i_t = \sum_{j=1}^{n} a_j^{(1)} i_{t-j} + \sum_{j=1}^{n} \beta_j^{(1)} P_{t-j}. \tag{A9}$$

$$P_j = \sum_{j=1}^{n} c_j^{(1)} i_{t-j} + \sum_{j=1}^{n} d_j^{(1)} P_{t-j}. \tag{A10}$$

(Note that the rationale for estimating equations (A7) and (A9) in addition to (A8) and (A10) is close to the model for price expectations implicit in the latter two equations.) Further, if expectations are rational, multi-span forecasts of both the real rate of interest and the rate of inflation must be generated recursively, with the optimal forecasts of these two variables being substituted for the as yet unrealized values of the respective series. As Modigliani and Shiller demonstrate, this use of the 'chain principle' of forecasting enables the multispan forecasts also to be expressed as functions of the observed histories of the real interest rate and the rate of inflation. The weights used to generate the rational forecast of inflation in period $t + i$ ($c_j^{(i)}$ and $d_j^{(i)}$) are complicated functions of the four sets of parameters estimated for equations (A9) and (A10). Since the forecast of inflation over any multi-period horizon can be expressed as the geometric average of the series of corresponding one period forecasts, one can use these rational forecasts of the one period rates of inflation expected to prevail in period $t + 1$, $t + 2$, and so on to construct appropriate multi-period forecasts. These multi-period forecasts can then be matched to the maturities of the several interest rates employed in the empirical tests of the alternative models.

Finally, one ought to consider the implications of imposing rationality on the price expectations variables to be used in the empirical tests of the alternative models of the determinants of nominal interest rates. The assumption that market forecasts of inflation are rational is eminently reasonable from *a priori* considerations. In particular, this assumption draws support from the expanding empirical literature (see, for example, Fama, 1970; Fama *et al.*, 1969; Pesando, 1974) which supports the claim that *equity markets* are efficient. Efficiency, in the context of this literature, is equated with the proposition that stock prices fully reflect all information (current and anticipated) relevant to the determination of common stock prices. The growing evidence that the expectations relevant to stock price determination are (in effect) rational serves to cast doubt on the proposition that market forecasts of inflation might not be rational. The relevance of the efficient capital markets literature is further enhanced by the recognition that the variance in nominal interest rates largely reflects the variance in price expectations, implying the existence of profitable arbitrage opportunities to individual investors who fully exploit available information regarding the future course of inflation: i.e., to individual investors who form rational price expectations.

Empirical results

Before conducting the (two sets of) formal tests of the impact of price expectations on nominal interest rates, one must first construct the synthetic price expectations series as previously described. To construct these series, equations (A9) and (A10) were estimated using quarterly data on the 90-day Treasury Bill rate and the rate on inflation (as measured by the Consumer Price Index) for the sample period 1959:1 – 1971:2. The choice of the beginning date for the regressions was dictated by the desire to exclude the period prior to mid-1955, a transitional period in Canadian monetary history which witnessed the development of the first meaningful money market in Canada. The terminal date was dictated by the fact that Modigliani and Shiller (1973, 23-5) demonstrate that the imposition of wage and price controls in 1971 affected the mechanism by which price expectations in the United States were formed. Given the close economic ties between Canada and the United States, this disruption in the expectations-generating mechanism is likely to have occurred in Canada as well. The first terms in the summation expressions in equations (A9) and (A10) were entered separately in the regression equations, while the remaining lag coefficients were constrained to lie along third-order polynomials with 16 quarter lags. This approach permits one to impose the constraints suggested by Modigliani and Shiller (1973, 34-5); i.e., $\sum_j a_j^{(1)} = \sum_j d_j^{(1)} = 1$ and $\sum_j \beta_j^{(1)} = \sum_j c_j^{(1)} = 0$. The criterion for choosing the degree and length of the lag-generating polynomials, as suggested by Schmidt and Waud (1973), was the minimization of the standard error of the regression. The rational forecasts of inflation over alternative time horizons were then constructed using the methods outlined in section II and the coefficients estimated for equations (A9) and (A10).

One should emphasize at this point the importance of the possible break in the mechanism by which price expectations in Canada were formed following the imposition of wage and price controls in the United States. As noted, this fact dictated the terminal date for the estimation of the equations necessary to construct the synthetic price expectations series. The result also suggests the possibility of discontinuity, in terms of their adequacy as a measure of the mechanism by which inflationary expectations are formed, of the distributed lag proxies for price expectations. In view of these problems, regressions were performed for two sample periods: (1) 1959:1 – 1971:2, and (2) 1959:1 – 1974:4. As noted, *a priori* considerations suggest that greater weight be attached to the former results, while the desire to exploit the more recent data – quite rich in terms of the volatility of both interest rates and observed rates of inflation – required the estimation of the latter.

Finally, one seeks a measure of the impact on nominal interest rates of variations in the degree of uncertainty with which price expectations are held, hereafter referred to as inflation risk. For empirical purposes, inflation risk was approximated by an eight-quarter moving standard deviation of the difference between the (one quarter) inflation rate and the rational forecast (i.e., extracted from the synthetic price expectations series for one quarter forecasts) of this rate made one quarter previously.

To sum up, two measures of price expectations and one measure of inflation risk have been constructed in an attempt to measure the impact of both expected and unexpected (embodied in the variable to measure inflation risk) inflation on nominal interest rates. These variables were then included in the Y-K, C-S, and J-L models of the determinants of nominal interest rates, and the resulting regressions performed for two sample periods. For comparability with the synthetic price expectations series, the length of the lag in the distributed lag proxies was set equal to 16 quarters. The distributed lag coefficients were estimated using a third-degree polynomial (see Almon, 1965) subject to a zero end-point constraint.

The dependent variable in the regressions were the 90-day Treasury Bill rate, and the one-to-three year, three-to-five year, five-to-ten year and ten-year-and-over Government of Canada bond rates. The Y-K, C-S, and J-L models were then estimated for the two sample periods cited earlier in the text. Since our interest is concerned only with the role of the price expectations and inflation risk variables, only the coefficients of these variables together with the $\bar{R}^2$ for the corresponding equation are presented in Tables A1-A4. One need only note that in every case the additional variables in the respective models were always correctly signed, although they were not always significant. (For an illustrative set of the complete results for each of these models, see Pesando, 1976).

As noted previously, economic considerations suggest that greater weight be attached to the rational expectations (Table A1) and distributed lag (Table A2) results for the period 1959:1-1971:2, and these estimates thus provide the basis for most of the remarks contained below.

In general, the regression results suggest two important conclusions regarding the impact of inflation on nominal interest rates: (1) price expectations do appear to be 'fully' (i.e., enter with coefficient of unity) incorporated into nominal yields, and (2) inflation risk, except for the shortest maturity considered, is borne by the investor, since increased uncertainty with regard to the expected inflation rate, *ceteris paribus*, serves to reduce nominal interest

TABLE A.1

Estimates of the impact of price expectations and inflation risk on nominal interest rates: rational price expectations, 1959:1–1971:2

| | Model of the determinants of nominal interest rates | | | | | | | | |
| | Yohe-Karnosky | | | Carr-Smith | | | Jenkins-Lim | | |
Interest rate	PEXP	RISK	$\bar{R}^2$	PEXP	RISK	$\bar{R}^2$	PEXP	RISK	$\bar{R}^2$
90-day treasury bills	0.89 (0.10)		0.60	0.86 (0.10)		0.63	1.02 (0.11)		0.80
	1.01 (0.12)	0.83 (0.55)	0.60	0.97 (0.11)	0.74 (0.53)	0.63	1.05 (0.11)	0.41 (0.44)	0.81
1-3 year gov't bond	0.94 (0.11)		0.59	0.93 (0.10)		0.64	1.34 (0.11)		0.84
	1.08 (0.14)	−0.89 (0.50)	0.54	1.09 (0.13)	−0.95 (0.46)	0.61	1.50 (0.14)	−2.24 (0.48)	0.81
3.5 year gov't bond	0.99 (0.09)		0.72	0.99 (0.08)		0.75	1.30 (0.08)		0.87
	1.05 (0.10)	−0.86 (0.40)	0.68	1.07 (0.10)	−0.92 (0.37)	0.72	1.44 (0.11)	−2.11 (0.40)	0.85
5-10 year gov't bond	1.01 (0.08)		0.78	1.01 (0.07)		0.79	1.30 (0.08)		0.89
	1.10 (0.08)	−0.63 (0.33)	0.79	1.11 (0.08)	−0.67 (0.31)	0.80	1.43 (0.09)	−1.72 (0.33)	0.90
10 year and over gov't bond	0.91 (0.07)		0.76			0.77	1.19 (0.08)		0.84
	1.03 (0.07)	−0.33 (0.26)	0.83	1.03 (0.07)	−0.34 (0.26)	0.83	1.30 (0.08)	−1.20 (0.30)	0.90

NOTES: (1) PEXP represents the rational price expectations variable whose time horizon is identical to the maturity of the indicated interest rate. (2) RISK represents the degree of uncertainty with which price expectations are held and is approximated by an eight-quarter moving standard deviation of the difference between the (one quarter) inflation rate and the forecast of this rate made one quarter previously. These forecasts are drawn from the synthetic price expectations (one quarter) series. Bracketed figures are standard errors. All regressions exhibit significant positive serial correlation.

TABLE A.2

Estimates of the impact of price expectations and inflation risk on nominal interest rates: distributed lag expectations proxies, 1959:1–1971:2

Model of the determinants of nominal interest rates

Interest rate	Yohe-Karmosky			Carr-Smith			Jenkins-Lim		
	PEXP	RISK	$\bar{R}^2$	PEXP	RISK	$\bar{R}^2$	PEXP	RISK	$\bar{R}^2$
90-day treasury bills	0.95		0.64	0.95		0.71	1.10		0.90
	(0.14)			(0.07)			(0.10)		
	1.02	−0.54	0.68	1.07	−0.43	0.74	1.20	−1.15	0.91
	(0.23)	(0.66)		(0.21)	(0.57)		(0.14)	(0.48)	
1-3 year gov't bond	0.96		0.78	0.97		0.84	1.07		0.91
	(0.09)			(0.08)			(0.09)		
	1.06	−0.64	0.82	1.03	−0.56	0.86	1.17	−1.22	0.93
	(0.15)	(0.54)		(0.13)	(0.47)		(0.11)	(0.38)	
3-5 year gov't bond	1.00		0.84	1.01		0.86	1.10		0.90
	(0.07)			(0.07)			(0.09)		
	1.00	−0.17	0.85	0.98	−0.13	0.86	1.17	−0.95	0.91
	(0.13)	(0.46)		(0.12)	(0.44)		(0.11)	(0.40)	
5-10 year gov't bond	1.05		0.89	1.05		0.90	1.10		0.91
	(0.07)			(0.06)			(0.13)		
	1.02	−0.28	0.88	1.01	−0.26	0.88	1.16	−0.95	0.92
	(0.11)	(0.41)		(0.11)	(0.41)		(0.11)	(0.38)	
10 year and over gov't bond	1.00		0.88	1.00		0.87	1.01		0.88
	(0.06)			(0.06)			(0.09)		
	0.91	−0.41	0.83	0.91	−0.42	0.82	1.08	−1.14	0.89
	(0.13)	(0.45)		(0.13)	(0.46)		(0.12)	(0.41)	

NOTES: (1) Sum of the distributed lag coefficients, which indicates the impact of price expectations under the identifying restriction that the sum of the lag weights in the expectations-generating mechanism equals unity. See text for elaboration. (2) See notes to Table A1. (3) Bracketed figures are standard errors. All regressions exhibit significant positive serial correlation.

TABLE A.3

Estimates of the impact of price expectations and inflation risk on nominal interest rates: rational price expectations, 1959:1–1974:4

	Model of the determinants of nominal interest rates								
	Yohe-Karnosky			Carr-Smith			Jenkins-Lim		
Interest rate	PEXP	RISK	$\bar{R}^2$	PEXP	RISK	$\bar{R}^2$	PEXP	RISK	$\bar{R}^2$
90-day treasury bills	0.41 (0.06)		0.39	0.41 (0.06)		0.42	0.53 (0.10)		0.47
	0.44 (0.07)	-0.55 (0.67)	0.40	0.43 (0.07)	-0.54 (0.66)	0.43	0.67 (0.12)	-1.34 (0.70)	0.55
1-3 year gov't bond	0.54 (0.08)		0.39	0.54 (0.08)		0.41	0.47 (0.13)		0.42
	0.56 (0.10)	-0.27 (0.63)	0.40	0.57 (0.10)	-0.28 (0.61)	0.41	0.47 (0.21)	-0.01 (0.83)	0.41
3-5 year gov't bond	0.66 (0.07)		0.59	0.67 (0.07)		0.61	0.70 (0.26)		0.60
	0.72 (0.08)	-0.61 (0.48)	0.59	0.73 (0.08)	-0.64 (0.47)	0.61	0.99 (0.17)	-1.36 (0.62)	0.63
5-10 year gov't bond	0.71 (0.06)		0.72	0.72 (0.06)		0.73	0.79 (0.09)		0.73
	0.77 (0.07)	-0.67 (0.39)	0.73	0.78 (0.06)	-0.69 (0.39)	0.74	1.14 (0.13)	-1.72 (0.48)	0.78
10 year and over gov't bond	0.70 (0.04)		0.80	0.70 (0.04)		0.80	0.77 (0.07)		0.80
	0.74 (0.05)	-0.45 (0.31)	0.80	0.74 (0.05)	-0.46 (0.31)	0.80	1.02 (0.10)	-1.23 (0.39)	0.83

NOTES: (1) See notes to Table A1. (2) Bracketed figures are standard errors. All regressions exhibit significant positive serial correlation.

TABLE A.4

Estimates of the impact of price expectations and inflation risk on nominal interest rates: distributed lag lag expectations proxies, 1959:1–1974:4

Model of the determinants of nominal interest rates

Interest rate	Yohe-Karnosky PEXP	RISK	$\bar{R}^2$	Carr-Smith PEXP	RISK	$\bar{R}^2$	Jenkins-Lim PEXP	RISK	$\bar{R}^2$
90-day treasury bills	0.68		0.59	0.68		0.61	0.82		0.73
	(0.14)			(0.13)			(0.13)		
	0.85	−1.42	0.62	0.85	−1.41	0.65	1.24	−2.60	0.83
	(0.14)	(0.59)		(0.13)	(0.57)		(0.11)	(0.44)	
1-3 year gov't bond	0.72		0.74	0.72		0.76	0.76		0.79
	(0.10)			(0.09)			(0.10)		
	0.84	−1.06	0.76	0.84	−1.05	0.78	1.01	−1.59	0.83
	(0.10)	(0.51)		(0.09)	(0.39)		(0.10)	(0.39)	
3-5 year gov't bond	0.71		0.78	0.71		0.78	0.73		0.79
	(0.08)			(0.08)			(0.09)		
	0.81	−0.87	0.79	0.81	−0.87	0.80	0.93	−1.21	0.82
	(0.08)	(0.36)		(0.08)	(0.35)		(0.10)	(0.38)	
5-10 year gov't bond	0.77		0.84	0.77		0.84	0.77		0.85
	(0.07)			(0.07)			(0.08)		
	0.87	−0.90	0.86	0.87	−0.89	0.86	0.94	−1.08	0.87
	(0.07)	(0.30)		(0.09)	(0.29)		(0.08)	(0.32)	
10 year and over gov't bond	0.73		0.81	0.73		0.80	0.70		0.80
	(0.07)			(0.07)			(0.08)		
	0.80	−0.56	0.81	0.80	−0.36	0.80	0.77	−0.40	0.80
	(0.07)	(0.32)		(0.08)	(0.32)		(0.09)	(0.36)	

NOTES: (1) See notes to Table A1. (2) Bracketed figures are standard errors. All regressions exhibit significant positive serial correlation.

rates. From an institutional viewpoint, an increase in inflation risk appears to encourage borrowers into the short-term market, forcing them to pay (slightly) higher rates, while the concomitant reduction in the demand for long-term financing results *ceteris paribus* in lower long-term yields.

From a statistical viewpoint, several other aspects of the empirical results merit comment. First, the explanatory power of the several models increases as the maturities of the interest rates increase, indicating that price expectations (in particular) are a more dominant force in shaping long-term relative to short-term interest rates. Second, all equations exhibit significant positive serial correlation, thus suggesting the possibility of misspecification in each of the Y-K, C-S, and J-L models. The second problem suggests the importance of re-examining the results in a framework which attempts to deal with the serial correlation in the residuals. To this end, the equations in Table A1 were re-estimated using the Hildreth-Lu procedure (1960). In general, the coefficients of the price expectations variables were lower than those presented in Table A1, but not sufficiently so as to lead one to alter the basic conclusion regarding their 'full' incorporation. The coefficient of the price expectations variable in the J-L model for the long-term government bond rate, to draw an example from the higher end of the estimated coefficients, was equal to 1.11 in the Hildreth-Lu regression compared to 1.30 in the ordinary least squares regression. In addition, the inflation risk variables were less significant, indicating that inflation risk – at least as measured in our estimates – had a much less important impact on nominal interest rates.

Examination of the results for the extended 1959:1-1974:4 period reveals the anticipated deterioration in the performance of the Y-K, C-S and J-L models, a deterioration likely to be due to the limitations of the price expectations proxies. Note that these results are uniformly inferior (lower $\bar{R}^2$ and lower DW) to their counterparts in Tables A1 and A2. Of particular note is the fairly dramatic reduction in the coefficients of the key price expectations variable in all of the estimated equations. These results, in general, would tend to support the conclusion that price expectations are *not* 'fully' incorporated into nominal interest rates. This conclusion, which conflicts with the one drawn earlier on the basis of the 1959:1-1971:2 results, merits serious qualification in view of the probable limitation of the two sets of price expectations proxies. The imposition of wage-price controls in the United States in the third quarter of 1971 and its impact on the expectations-generating mechanism has already been noted. Further, there exists the possibility that the market has been discounting the extraordinary high rates of inflation which prevailed (say) in 1974 as transitory, a possibility that distributed lags could not capture due to their inherent inflexibility in this regard. In summary, however, one must acknowledge that the estimates obtained for the larger sample period do cast a shadow over the conclusions extracted from the earlier results. The results for the longer period indicate that either (1) price expectations are not 'fully' incorporated into nominal interest rates, or (2) price expectations are not adequately proxied in the extended period. The latter is the preferred interpretation, but even its acceptance raises concern about the validity of the alternative price expectations in the shorter period as well.

Finally, the extended results continue to support the earlier conclusions regarding the impact of inflation risk, including the conclusion that the importance of the effect is not great. In general, these results suggest the importance of attempting to obtain more flexible measures of price expectations in order to obtain more reliable empirical results.

To sum up, the empirical results support the tentative conclusion that, *ceteris paribus,* a one per cent change in price expectations will produce a corresponding one per cent change in nominal interest rates. The implication of this result is that all investors whose marginal tax bracket is not zero suffer a decline in real after-tax returns whenever price expectations – and hence nominal interest rates – increase. The fact that nominal interest rates do not adjust sufficiently to prevent an increase in expected inflation from lowering real after-tax returns is presumably due to the fact that many participants in the Canadian capital market, including most financial intermediaries, have no alternative but to commit a major portion of their investment funds to fixed-income securities. As a result, the adjustment process by which price expectations are incorporated into nominal interest rates is largely limited to demand factors. Because the investment income of private pension plans is tax exempt, however, the fact that each one per cent rise in price expectations leads to a one per cent increase in nominal interest rates is sufficient to leave the real after-tax return of newly-acquired fixed-income securities unaffected by changes in inflationary expectations.

II INFLATION AND THE RATE OF RETURN ON EQUITIES

As noted in the text, the Pension Benefits Act of 1965 appears to accept the conventional wisdom that common stocks are an adequate 'inflation hedge' by virtue of its provisions which permit up to 100 per cent of the funds of non-insured plans or insured plans using the segregated fund principle to be invested in common stocks. The Act, in effect, invites private pension plans to avail themselves of the presumed tendency of the nominal yield on equities to exceed the rate of inflation, at least over sufficiently long holding periods.

The issue of whether or not common stocks are an adequate 'inflation hedge' is central to an understanding of the viability of private pension plans in an inflationary climate. Inflation, as noted previously, poses two fundamental challenges to the ability of private pension plans to provide adequate retirement incomes. For final earnings plans (which effectively protect the real value of employees' pensions *during their working years*), inflation may produce sharp increases in experience deficiencies which employers may or may not be able to finance out of operating earnings. In addition, inflation erodes the real value of pension benefits during employees' retirement years unless those benefits are fully indexed, an event which is quite rare in Canada. If equities represent an adequate 'inflation hedge' (appropriately defined), and ignoring for the moment the issue of the volatility of returns, then a private pension plan which is fully invested in equities will eliminate *both* of these problems. Experience deficiencies will not occur in an inflationary climate, *and* pension plans will be able to index pension benefits and retain their actuarial soundness. In essence, all inflation – whether expected or unexpected – could be anticipated in the context of the management of private pension plans.

The empirical issue of the extent to which equities provide a hedge against inflation is thus an important one in the context of the operation of private pension plans. An examination of this issue must logically begin with an appropriate definition of the term 'inflation hedge.' This definitional issue is important and precedes the analysis of the empirical work.

Equities as an 'inflation hedge'
One way to answer the question of whether or not equities represent an adequate hedge against inflation is to define equities as an adequate hedge if their nominal rate of return exceeds the average rate of inflation, at least over holding periods sufficiently long as to smooth the inherent fluctuations in these yields. This definition is implicit, for example, in the recent work of Cagan (1974), who finds empirical support for the hypothesis that equities represent an adequate inflation hedge in his comparison of the return on equities (exclusive of dividend yields) with the actual rate of inflation for all countries which report such data to the International Monetary Fund. This definition also appears to be the one implicit in the design of the Pension Benefits Act of 1965, which reflects the then conventional wisdom that equities do represent an adequate inflation hedge as so defined. (For statements embodying this assumption, see Ontario, 1961).

The above definition, however, is not really very satisfactory. Even if common stocks are an adequate inflation hedge as so defined (and economic theory indicates that they should be), a number of important issues remain unanswered. Is the real rate of return on equities likely to rise (fall) in a period of accelerating (decelerating) inflation? Are the long-term (positive) real returns larger or smaller because of inflation than they otherwise would have been?

Further, are the answers to the above questions sensitive to the issue of whether or not the observed inflation is expected or unexpected? The answers to these questions are extremely important if one seeks to be able to predict the impact of *changes* in the rate of inflation on the real return on equities and ultimately to provide a better perspective on the extent to which a pension fund which is fully invested in equities effectively anticipates inflation. The evidence cited by Cagan only indicates that the multiplicity of factors which govern the yield on common stocks have interacted in such a way as to provide, over sufficiently long periods of time, positive real returns. The evidence provides no insight into the impact of inflation *per se* on the real returns provided by a diversified portfolio of common stocks.

Consider first the question of whether or not the real return on equities should be invariant with respect to the realized rate of inflation. If these real returns are unaffected, one might then choose to define equities as an adequate hedge against inflation. As Lintner (1973, 1975) observes, classical economic theory has long presumed that the real return on equities is unaffected by either inflationary or deflationary changes in the price level. This presumption, in turn, rests on three additional presuppositions: (1) the real returns to the owners of capital goods will be invariant to the general price level, since these returns reflect existing production functions and factor proportions which are insensitive to the general level of prices; (2) the real market value (V) of capital goods will equal the flow of these real returns (R) discounted by the real interest rate (i); and (3) the real interest rate will also be invariant to the general level of prices since it simply equilibriates the marginal productivity of capital goods with consumers' marginal rate of time preference. One can write this result as follows:

$$V = \sum_{t=1}^{\infty} [R_t / (1+i)^t].$$ (A11)

Since the real value of the ownership claims is thus invariant to the price level, their nominal value will vary in direct proportion to the general price level. Further, the real value of these ownership claims will be invariant to expected inflation ($P*$) as well, since the higher nominal value of the flow of returns will be discounted by a nominal interest rate which also adjusts upward in response to the higher expected rate of inflation:

$$V = \sum_{t=1}^{\infty} [(R_t) (1+P*)^t / (1+i)^t (1+P*)^t] = \sum_{t=1}^{\infty} [R_t/(1+i)^t]. \quad \text{(A12)}$$

Finally, if the ownership of the underlying capital goods is partially financed by debt, the real returns to the owners of the capital goods will rise in a period of unexpected inflation. This result follows from the fact that the real market value of the outstanding debt falls while the real value of the (levered) equity rises by an amount equal to the decline in the real value of the debt.

In summary, classical economic theory predicts that the real value of unlevered equity should be invariant with respect to inflation, regardless of whether the inflation is expected or unexpected. Further, the real value of levered equity should be invariant with respect to expected inflation and should increase in periods of unexpected inflation. This latter argument, in turn, is easily rephrased in more modern terms by saying that the real value of equity is unaffected by expected inflation, but will rise (fall) in periods of unexpected inflation if the firm is a net debtor (creditor).

Financial analysts, however, are quick to point out several important qualifications to the neutrality conclusions of classical economic analysis. Both the tax requirement that depreciation on fixed assets be calculated at historical rather than at replacement cost and the 'phantom' nature of the added accounting profits created by evaluating inventories at average costs or by *fifo* rather than *lifo* methods, for example, serve *ceteris paribus* to reduce the real return on capital goods when inflation accelerates. Numerous other issues can be raised in this context (Lintner, 1975, 272-6; Branch, 1974, 49) but the thrust of their message can be summarized succinctly: the conclusions of the classical analysis regarding the neutrality of the real return on equities with respect to inflation are, at best, problematic and should be the subject of additional empirical research.

Indeed, recent attempts to explore the link between inflation and the real return on common stocks universally suggest that equities are *not* an adequate inflation hedge since (1) the real return on equities is negatively correlated with observed inflation, and (2) the real return on equities is negatively correlated with *both* expected and unexpected inflation. Lintner (1973), Branch (1974), and Nelson (1976) all obtain econometric estimates which indicate, in effect, that the real return on equities, *ceteris paribus,* falls when inflation accelerates. Further, both Nelson (1976) and Body (1976) obtain evidence which suggests that the real return on equities is negatively correlated to *both* expected and unexpected inflation. The latter authors, in particular, are rather disturbed by their conclusions, but find that their conclusions are not altered in the context of alternative specifications, alternative holding periods, and alternative sample periods. One should also emphasize that these results are *not* unique to the post world war II period. Lintner's results, for example, were obtained using annual data for the full 1900-71 period. A summary of the data, sample periods and results of these studies appears in Table A.5.

The importance of these tentative conclusions cannot be overemphasized. If true, they would indicate that a pension fund which is fully invested in equities

TABLE A.5

Prior empirical studies of the impact of inflation on the real returns of common stocks

Investigator	Data and Sample Period	Conclusions
1. Body (1976)	Monthly, quarterly and annual United States data, 1953-72	Both expected and unexpected inflation depress real returns
2. Branch (1975)	Twenty-two countries, annual data, 1953-69	Realized inflation depresses real returns
3. Lintner (1973)	Annual United States data, 1900-71	Realized inflation depresses real returns
4. Nelson (1976)	Monthly United States data, 1953-74	Both expected and unexpected inflation depress real returns

will incur experience deficiencies if the rate of inflation increases, independent of whether the higher rate of inflation is expected or unexpected. In addition, they would indicate that such a pension plan, if actuarially sound under the assumption of a zero rate of inflation, could not remain actuarially sound and provide full indexation of benefits during employees' retirement years in an inflationary climate.

The importance of these tentative findings thus suggests that they merit examination in the Canadian context as well. The framework adopted in order to explore these issues mirrors the one developed by Body (1976). This framework is sketched briefly below and is followed by an analysis of the empirical results.

The framework of the investigation
Implicit in the preceding discussion are three alternative (but not independent) definitions of the term 'inflation hedge' as it pertains to common stocks: (1) equities are an inflation hedge if their real return is either invariant or positively related to the realized rate of inflation; (2) equities are an inflation hedge if their real return is either invariant or positively related to both expected and unexpected inflation; (3) equities are an inflation hedge if their real return is either invariant or positively related to unexpected inflation, on the maintained hypothesis that the real rate of return must be invariant with respect to expected inflation. Each of these three definitions offers some (independent) perspective on the impact of inflation on a pension fund which is fully invested in equities and therefore merits analysis in an empirical context.

The three definitions noted above suggest three alternative specifications in which to examine the relationship between inflation and the real rate of return on equities:

$$\Gamma_t = \alpha_0 + \alpha_1 \dot{P}_t + \epsilon_t; \tag{A13}$$

$$\Gamma_t = B_0 + B_1 \left(_t\dot{P}_{t-1}{}^*\right) + B_2 \left(\dot{P}_t - {}_t\dot{P}_{t-1}{}^*\right) + \mu_t; \tag{A14}$$

$$\Gamma_t = c_0 + c_1 \left(\dot{P}_t - {}_t\dot{P}_{t-1}{}^*\right) + v_t; \tag{A15}$$

where: $\Gamma_t = N_t - \dot{P}_t$ (ex post return on equities in period t), $N_t = $ ex post nominal return on equities in period t, $\dot{P}_t = $ the rate of inflation in period t, ${}_t\dot{P}_{t-1}{}^* = $ the forecast made in period t-1 of the rate of inflation in period t, $\epsilon_t, \mu_t, v_t = $ error terms. The dependent variable in each of these specifications is the ex post return on equities during the holding-period t. The ex ante return, of course, is not observable. The presumption is that the realized return differs from the ex ante return by a random disturbance term, although the exact interpretation varies from one specification to the next. In the first, the impact of observed inflation on the realized real return on equities is explored, although no attempt is made to disentangle the (separate) contribution of expected and unexpected inflation (whose sum, of course, equals the actual inflation rate). This specification has the advantage of not requiring the construction of a proxy variable to measure inflationary expectations. The second specification does attempt to disentangle the separate roles for both expected and unexpected inflation. The third specification seeks only to identify the impact of unexpected inflation on the ex post real return on equities. In several ways, this specification is the most interesting. This final framework is consistent with the literature on efficient capital markets, which suggest that only unexpected changes in contemporary economic variables should bear a systematic relationship to realized returns on common stocks. The forecasting error term, in effect, decomposes the volatility of ex post real returns into the component associated with unexpected inflation and the component which is orthogonal to unexpected inflation.

One should note, in passing, that none of these specifications purports to offer a complete specification of the determinants of the real rate of return on equities. In general, the ex ante real return on equities is likely to exhibit very small variance relative to the observed variability in ex post returns. This hypothesis reflects, in part, the theoretical proposition that in equilibrium the ex ante risk-adjusted returns on holding wealth in alternative forms should be forced to equality. In this light, the tremendous variance in the realized return on equities compared (say) to the realized return on short-term bonds suggests the overwhelming importance of the impact on the former of random disturbances which reflect the net impact of all events which (1) influence equity returns, and (2) are unexpected, at least at the beginning of the holding period. Since only variables designed to measure the impact of inflation are included in these specifications, one must acknowledge the possibility that any statistical significance assigned to the relevant variables might reflect the impact on the realized returns of omitted variables which are correlated with the alternative measures of the impact of inflation. This caveat is an important one, but clearly there is no feasible way to (say) attempt to measure and incorporate into the alternative specifications unexpected changes in all the economic variables which may be relevant to the determination of the yield on common stocks.

Empirical results

In order to estimate the equations cited in the preceding section, one must have data on the nominal return over various holding periods of a representative index of common stocks, which would approximate the return available on a well-diversified portfolio. Monthly price relatives for the Toronto Stock Exchange industrial index, compiled by the Faculty of Management Studies at the University of Toronto, proved to be satisfactory for this purpose. These price relatives, calculated both with and without the reinvestment of dividends, were available from 1956. The availability of these data on price relatives, which incorporate the changes in stock prices as well as their dividend yields, played a major role in determining the sample period for the regressions. The Consumer Price Index was chosen as the means of measuring inflation, while the synthetic expectations series created earlier by invoking the rational expectations hypothesis were employed as the appropriate measures of expected inflation. As noted previously, the usefulness of these synthetic series is somewhat suspect after the second quarter of 1971, reflecting the imposition of wage and price controls in the United States. As a result, all regressions were run for two sample periods: (1) as early as possible, given data availability constraints, to 1971:2; and (2) as early as possible to the latest quarter for which the data on price relatives were available. In addition, all regressions were run for both sets of price relatives; i.e., both with and without the reinvestment of dividends.

An additional issue is the choice of the length of the holding period in which to investigate the relationship between inflation and the rate of return on equities. On the one hand, the choice of a short holding period (e.g., one month or one quarter) permits one to work with a large number of independent observations, but is perhaps too short to be of great interest to pension plans who adopt substantially longer investment horizons. On the other hand, the choice of a longer holding period (e.g., several years) forces one either to work with a very small sample or to work with overlapping observations. The latter procedure, in turn, raises a number of econometric problems. As a compromise, all regressions were performed for three different holding periods: three months, two years, and four years. All regressions were performed with quarterly data, so that the two larger holding periods incorporate overlapping observations. The choice of the specific holding periods reflected the availability from the earlier work on interest rates of synehetic price expectations series for these time horizons.

Finally, one must acknowledge the problems associated with constructing appropriate measures of unexpected inflation, at least for the two longer holding periods. For the three-month holding period, unexpected inflation can be proxied by the difference between the observed rate of inflation during the quarter and the rational forecast of this three-month rate of inflation made at the beginning of the quarter. For both the longer-term holding periods, however, the problem is more complex. Consider, for example, the two-year holding period. One could proxy unexpected inflation by subtracting from the average inflation rate over the two-year period, the rational forecast of this two-year inflation rate made two years earlier. This procedure, however, involves the presumption that the market's expectation of inflation did not change in response to new information regarding (for example) the observed rate of inflation which would have become available as the period progressed. Clearly, this presumption would appear to be suspect. At the other extreme, one could proxy unexpected inflation by subtracting from the average inflation rate during the two-year period, the average of the two-year forecasts of inflation made during this two-year period. This procedure would create a measure of unexpected inflation which would more closely approximate the tendency for the market to adjust its expectations regarding the future rate of inflation on the basis of new information as it becomes available. In fact, both procedures for proxying unexpected inflation were employed for the two longer holding periods. Since, perhaps surprisingly, the empirical results were not sensitive to the choice of the measure of unexpected inflation, only the results based on the first procedure described in the text are reported in this appendix.

The empirical results for the specifications cited in the text are presented in Table A6 (with re-investment of dividends) and Table A7 (without re-investment). Consider the first specification, which seeks to isolate the impact of the observed rate of inflation on the *ex post* real return on equities. The results cited in Tables A6 and A7 indicate a negative and significant relationship between these two variables, a result which is at odds with much of the conventional wisdom on the subject. One should note, however, that the high 't' statistics of the inflation variable in the regressions for the two longer holding periods merit qualification. The overlapping of observations in order to perform these regressions tends to generate artificial serial correlation which, in turn, imparts a

TABLE A.6

Real return on equities (with re-investment of dividends), expected and unexpected inflation

Holding period	CONSTANT	PEXP	ERROR	INFL	$\bar{R}^2$	DW	Sample period
3 months	16.58	−4.27	−3.66		0.09	1.77	1957:2-1971:2
	(1.79)	(1.16)	(2.10)				
	6.77		−3.32		0.06	1.74	1957:2-1971:2
	(1.78)		(1.93)				
	15.41			−3.74	0.07	1.77	1957:2-1971:2
	(2.77)			(2.27)			
	10.95	−1.50	−3.06		0.04	1.85	1957:2-1973:4
	(1.60)	(0.70)	(2.05)				
	6.81		−3.06		0.05	1.84	1959:2-1973:4
	(1.99)		(2.06)				
	13.67			−2.55	0.05	1.84	1959:2-1973:4
	(2.69)			(2.09)			
2 years	17.18	−4.69	−2.37		0.24	0.70	1959:1-1971:2
	(5.70)	(3.08)	(2.25)				
	8.80		−2.36		0.08	0.62	1951:1-1971:2
	(6.28)		(2.07)				
	14.90			−3.12	0.19	0.69	1959:1-1971:2
	(6.16)			(3.58)			
	11.09	−1.33	−1.41		0.04	0.64	1959:1-1973:4
	(4.80)	(1.37)	(1.35)				
	8.45		−1.64		0.03	0.64	1959:1-1973:4
	(6.52)		(1.59)				
	11.13			−1.36	0.06	0.63	1959:1-1973:4
	(5.26)			(2.12)			
4 years	18.29	−4.03	−3.81		0.58	0.84	1961:1-1971:2
	(7.82)	(3.03)	(7.02)				
	11.62		−3.59		0.48	0.74	1961:1-1971:2
	(13.36)		(6.09)				
	18.00			−3.83	0.58	0.84	1961:1-1971:2
	(12.44)			(7.42)			
	15.49	−2.32	−3.55		0.54	0.88	1961:1-1973:4
	(10.16)	(3.26)	(6.95)				
	11.15		−3.63		0.45	0.78	1961:1-1973:4
	(13.77)		(6.53)				
	16.58			−3.12	0.53	0.83	1961:1-1973:4
	(12.68)			(7.65)			

NOTE: PEXP denotes the expected inflation rate; ERROR denotes the error (actual less expected) in forecasting the inflation rate; INFL denotes the actual rate of inflation. See text for amplification. Bracketed figures are 't' statistics.

TABLE A.7

Real return on equities (without re-investment of dividends), expected and unexpected inflation

Holding period	CONSTANT	PEXP	ERROR	INFL	$\bar{R}^2$	DW	Sample period
3 months	13.34	−4.36	−3.64		0.05	1.76	1957:2-1971:2
	(1.45)	(1.20)	(2.11)				
	3.30		−3.29		0.05	1.74	1957:2-1971:2
	(0.87)		(1.93)				
	11.93			−3.74	0.07	1.77	1957:2-1971:2
	(2.16)			(2.29)			
	5.39	−0.54	−3.18		0.04	1.80	1957:2-1973:3
	(0.76)	(0.23)	(2.14)				
	3.95		−3.19		0.05	1.80	1957:2-1973:3
	(1.15)		(2.16)				
	10.06			−2.39	0.04	1.78	1957:2-1973:3
	(1.99)			(1.94)			
2 years	13.09	−4.60	−2.30		0.22	0.69	1959:2-1971:2
	(4.63)	(3.22)	(2.33)				
	4.87		−2.30		0.07	0.61	1959:2-1971:2
	(3.68)		(2.13)				
	10.84			−3.04	0.22	0.69	1959:2-1971:2
	(4.76)			(3.72)			
	7.71	−1.63	−1.35		0.05	0.61	1959:2-1973:3
	(3.24)	(1.56)	(1.37)				
	4.52		−1.58		0.03	0.60	1959:2-1973:3
	(3.64)		(1.60)				
	7.51			−1.49	0.07	0.61	1959:2-1973:3
	(3.59)			(2.26)			
4 years	13.16	−3.80	−3.52		0.58	0.83	1961:1-1971:2
	(6.39)	(3.24)	(7.36)				
	6.87		−3.32		0.48	0.72	1961:1-1971:2
	(8.85)		(6.29)				
	12.79			−3.55	0.59	0.83	1961:2-1971:2
	(10.02)			(7.80)			
	10.82	−2.36	−3.33		0.56	0.86	1961:1-1973:3
	(7.74)	(3.57)	(7.25)				
	6.42		−3.34		0.45	0.73	1961:1-1973:3
	(8.74)		(6.53)				
	11.73			−3.01	0.56	0.82	1961:1-1973:3
	(9.91)			(7.97)			

NOTE: See notes to Table A.6 for variable definitions. Bracketed figures are 't' statistics.

downward bias to the standard errors of the estimated coefficients, and hence an upward bias to the calculated 't' statistics. The very low Durbin-Watson statistics provide strong evidence of the presence of serial correlation. No attempt was made to eliminate the serial correlation, however, since most procedures – such as the one suggested by Hildreth and Lu (1960) – are relevant only for the case of first-order serial correlation, while the nature of the overlapping observations suggests the presence of higher-order serial correlation as well. Note also that the estimated coefficients are still unbiased in spite of the presence of the pronounced serial correlation. In short, in spite of the above qualification, one can extract from these results the tentative conclusion that an increase in the rate of inflation, *ceteris paribus*, is associated with a reduction in the real return on equities. Note, in this regard, that the conclusion holds for both sets of price relatives.

The second specification permits one to isolate the impact of both expected and unexpected inflation on the real rate of return on equities. The results, again, are somewhat surprising, but not inconsistent with the recent United States studies cited earlier. In particular, expected as well as unexpected inflation is always negatively – and often significantly – related to the real return on equities. This result indicates that the negative association noted previously between observed inflation and the real rate of return on equities is not attributable solely to the unexpected component of observed inflation. One must, as before, interpret the 't' statistics in the regressions for the two longer holding periods with caution, but the tentative conclusion that both expected and unexpected inflation exert a depressing influence on the real return on common stocks appears to be warranted. Note, as before, that the explanatory power of the alternative regressions increases with the length of the holding period, a result which undoubtedly reflects the decreased volatility of realized returns when a longer unit of observation is adopted. Again, all results are similar for both sets of price relatives.

The specifications which focus solely on the relationship between real equity returns and unexpected inflation indicate an inverse relationship as well. As before, and especially for the three-month holding period, the explanatory power of the equations is low. This result serves to emphasize both the inherent volatility of common stock prices as well as the fact that the alternative specifications are not complete models of the determinants of the real return on equities.

Finally, one should note that the presence, in effect, of the observed inflation rate on both sides of the equations in these three specifications does not impart a bias to the estimated coefficients. Re-estimating the first two specifications with the nominal return on equities as the dependent variable, for example, would only result in the coefficients of the actual inflation rate, the expected inflation rate, and the forecasting error increasing by a value of one. Since the estimated coefficients in Tables A6 and A7 are all negative and greater than one in absolute value, these additional regressions would simply indicate that the nominal return on equities is negatively related to these variables as well.

To sum up, the empirical results suggest — albeit tentatively — that the real return on equities bears a negative relationship to both expected and unexpected inflation. This result, which tends to support the conclusions reached in several recent studies of the United States stock markets, suggests that the logic of assuming that a pension fund which is fully invested in equities should provide an adequate inflation hedge is highly suspect. Over sufficiently long periods of time, the real *ex post* return on equities should be positive, but this result cannot be used to support the conclusion that the nominal returns on equities rise sufficiently fast in periods of accelerating inflation to ensure that their real returns will not fall.

CONCLUSION

The key implication of the results presented in this appendix is that an increase in the rate of inflation, regardless of whether the increase is expected or unexpected, *cannot* be anticipated by managers of private pension plans, given the statutory constraints on the composition of their portfolios. In any period of accelerating inflation, one can predict that private pension plans — particularly those of the final earnings variety — will experience a sharp increase in experience deficiencies. The increase in experience deficiencies will represent the joint outcome of two factors: (1) the tendency for wages, in effect, to be a hedge against both expected and unexpected inflation (see DeMenil and Bhalla, 1975; Pesando and Sawyer, 1975), and (2) the tendency, already noted, for the real returns on portfolios consisting of bonds and/or equities, *ceteris paribus*, to fall in a period of accelerating inflation.

This point can be best illustrated by considering the impact of inflation on three representative types of pension fund portfolios: (1) a fund which is fully invested in equities (hereafter called the equity fund); (2) a fund which is fully invested in bonds of varying maturities (hereafter called the vintage bond portfolio); and (3) a fund which is fully invested in short-term bonds (hereafter called the short bond portfolio). The rationale for distinguishing two types of bond portfolios is, of course, related to the fact that expected inflation can be anticipated in a portfolio consisting entirely of short-term bonds, but not in a portfolio which includes bonds of varying maturities since such a portfolio would contain — at any point in time — bonds whose returns were fixed for

TABLE A.8

The impact of inflation on the experience deficiencies of pension plans according to the composition of their investment portfolios

Inflation	Experience deficiencies of		
	Equity portfolio	Vintage bond portfolio	Short bond portfolio
Increases/expected	Rise	Rise	Unchanged
Increases/unexpected	Rise	Rise	Rise
Decreases/expected	Fall	Fall	Unchanged
Decreases/unexpected	Fall	Fall	Fall

NOTE: These results will be most pronounced for final earnings plans and for flat benefit plans when the latter are continually revised as a by-product of labour-management negotiations.

substantial periods of time in the future. Although no pension funds, in fact, invest their funds predominantly in short-term bonds, this case does provide a useful perspective on the two more likely cases.

As a first approximation, one can assume that wages fully anticipate all inflation; i.e., a one per cent increase in the observed rate of inflation, regardless of whether the increase is expected or unexpected, *ceteris paribus,* leads to a one per cent increase in wages. Recent econometric research suggests that this assumption is perhaps too simple only in that it ignores the probable lags with which wages respond to inflation that was unexpected. Given this assumption, one can predict the impact of increasing or decreasing, expected or unexpected, inflation on the experience deficiencies of final earnings plans according to the composition of their investment portfolios in the manner summarized in Table A8.

Note that the two types of portfolios which are likely to be approximated by actual pension plans, the equity and the vintage bond portfolios, both experience increases (decreases) in experience deficiencies in periods of rising (falling) inflation. Clearly, any combination of these portfolios – which would best approximate the typical portfolio of most private pension plans – would exhibit a similar pattern. Only the short bond portfolio does not produce an increase in experience deficiencies in a period of rising inflation, but only if the inflation is expected.

The importance of these results cannot be overemphasized. They indicate, for example, that the sharp increase in the experience deficiencies of final earnings plans and (re-negotiated) flat benefit plans in recent years is quite predictable. Equally important, they indicate that this trend would be reversed if inflation were to slow in years ahead. Both results, at least superficially, would appear to provide an additional rationale for extending the amoritzation period for experience deficiencies, especially if such an extension were combined with a compulsory termination insurance scheme. The results also suggest the importance of considering the provision by the government of a fully indexed financial instrument. As noted previously, an indexed bond would enable managers of pension funds to anticipate inflation. An index bond would protect an employee's retirement benefits by (1) ensuring that pension plans would not suffer experience deficiencies during periods of rising inflation, and (2) enabling private plans to fully index pension benefits and yet remain actuarially sound. Since none of the portfolios described previously would permit a fund manager to fully anticipate inflation, none would permit a plan to protect the real pension benefits of employees during an inflationary period by the means outlined above.

The life simulation system

The simulation model generates the life histories of a sample of Canadians using Monte Carlo techniques. The sample population is augmented by those born in the future and those immigrating into Canada. The system allows one to examine income distribution effects of any government transfer program at one point in time or over a lifetime. It also allows one to predict aggregate taxes and benefits and to analyse the implications of changes in specific program parameters. The system consists of two parts: a program to generate the life histories, and a program to apply a particular public program to the individual life histories. These two programs will be discussed in turn.

THE GENERATION OF LIFE HISTORIES

The model is a further development of the micro simulation system developed by Dobell and Cohen (1975). A sample of individuals is created given the Canadian population in a base year cross classified by single years of age, sex, and province. Histories are generated so that the resulting sample will have the same age, sex, and provincial distribution in the base year (1966 for the analysis of the Canada Pension Plan) as the actual census distribution. Figures B.1, B.2, and B.3 summarize the model. Below is a description of how the variables are generated.

Marital status and school enrolment
Initial characteristics of the population age 18 and over are established through a Monte Carlo process. Marital status, educational achievement, spouse's age, and

Figure B1
Life Simulation System: Initial Characteristics

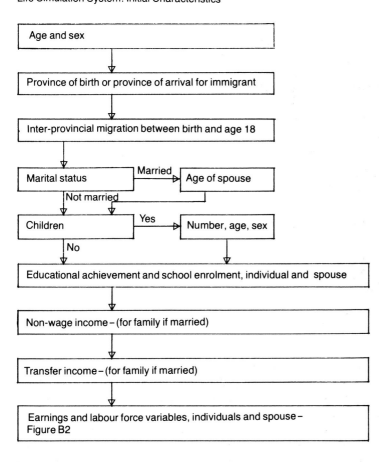

NOTE: Characteristics for individuals at age 18, for individuals 18 or
over in 1966, or new immigrants over age 18.

spouse's educational achievement are randomly assigned based on probability matrices developed by Cohen and Dobell (1975). Individuals are not matched up in families, but the characteristics of the spouse (male or female) are known. From the base year onward the probabilities of changing marital status, continuing in school, etc., are used to update the individual's record on an annual basis. When a divorce occurs the woman is assumed to have custody of the children. This part of the system was developed by Cohen and Dobell. The remainder of the program was developed by Rea and Cseh.

Figure B2
Life Simulation System: Labour Force Variables

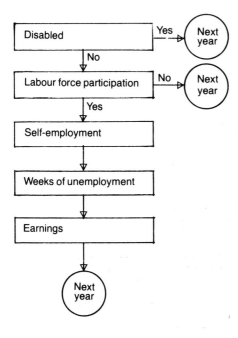

Number of children present in base year

The number of children in a family in the base year (or the number of children in a family that immigrates) was estimated from the 1972 Survey of Consumer Finances. First, the probability of having children aged 0-5 (or 6 to 15) was estimated using least squares regression, then the number of children was estimated for those with children. The dependent variables were age and education of husband and wife (if married) and province. In the simulation a random number determines whether or not a person has children present in the base year, and the number of children is predicted from the second equation. In order to determine the number of children an error term for the regression equation is drawn from a normal distribution with mean zero and standard deviation equal to the standard error of estimate for the regression. The normally distributed random variable (mean 0, variance 1) was obtained by summing twelve random numbers from a uniform distribution (with mean 0.5) and subtracting 6 (Hamming, 1962, 34, 389). The procedure was also applied to children aged 6 to 15. The ages of the children are arbitrarily assigned within the under 5 and 6 to 15 intervals. A maximum of 9 children is allowed.

Figure B3
Life Simulation System: Annual Update for Individual

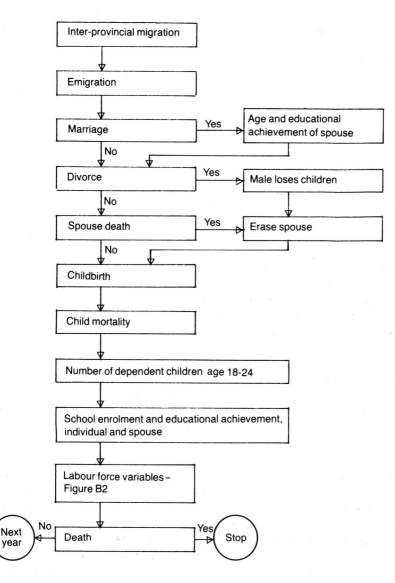

Number of dependent children

Since orphan benefits and disabled contributors children's benefits under the Canada Pension Plan are payable to children under 18 and single students under 25, the number of such children is updated each year. For those 18 and over the probability of leaving school was calculated from Statistics Canada school enrolment figures (Canada, 1972b, 162). Since over 81 per cent of those in University are not married, those in school are assumed to be dependents (Canada, 1972a). The annual school activity status for an individual, as opposed to his children, is predicted from a much more detailed transition matrix (Dobell and Cohen, 1975).

Birth

Age-specific fertility rates are applied annually to each female to predict whether children are born. Since there is a great deal of uncertainty about the future course of fertility rates, the program user can make his own assumptions about the future fertility rates. The program accepts five-year fertility rates which it interpolates for single years to match the 1971 pattern of birth rates within each five-year age bracket.

Those born after the base year enter the system as adults 18 years after birth. The number of births per province is recorded, and after allowing for inter-provincial migration before age 18 and child mortality, the 18-year-olds are treated just as someone in the base year. In other words they are assigned initial characteristics such as education and marital status at age 18.

Deaths

Sex specific mortality rates are specified by the user for five-year age brackets. These rates can be time-dependent so that greater longevity in the future can be hypothesized. In this study Statistics Canada forecasts were used (Canada, 1974a, 46).

Emigration

In recent years an estimated 60,000 people per year have left Canada (Canada, 1974a, 9). The age-sex distribution (single years of age) of these emigrants has been estimated by Gnanasekaran (1970). The probability of an individual leaving Canada is equal to the proportion of emigrants of his age and sex multiplied by the number of emigrants in the base year (60,000) and divided by the population in that age and sex category in the base year. This probability is kept constant over time, implying that if the Canadian population increases, an increasing absolute number of individuals will become emigrants. It is assumed that once an individual emigrates he does not return. He may, however, collect retirement benefits while abroad.

Immigration

The age-sex distribution of immigrants has also been estimated by Gnanasekaran (1970). This together with the 1971 to 1973 provincial distribution of immigrants (Canada, 1975c) allows one to introduce the immigrants into the system just as those in the base year are introduced. It is necessary to specify the number of immigrants entering per year. For this study a rate of 180,000 per year was assumed.

Interprovincial migration

Each year the individuals in the system face the probability of migrating between provinces. The 1971 census provides information on the age-sex composition of interprovincial migrants and the distribution of province of destination by province of origin in the 1966 to 1971 period (Canada, 1974d). These figures combined with estimates of the annual gross flow during this period (Canada, 1974a, 5) allow one to calculate the probability of migration by age, sex and province. For those who are migrants another probability distribution is used to determine the new province. The age and sex probabilities are assumed independent of the provincial migration propensities.

Disability

Disability is assigned to individuals in order to calculate their Canada Pension Plan disability benefits. The incidence of disability is taken from the Department of Insurance (Canada, 1973b, 66). It is assumed that once disabled one remains so for life. This is a reasonable assumption since relatively few of those collecting disability benefits under the CPP go back into the labour force.[1] Disability as well as labour force participation and other variables are assigned to the spouse as well as to the individual whose record is being examined (the 'sample individual').

Labour force participation

The probability of being in the labour force during the year (defined here as having worked during the year) was estimated from the 1972 Survey of Consumer Finances. Separate regressions were run for married men, married women, single men, and single women.[2] The independent variables are age, sex, education, province, presence of children, and school enrolment. The predicted probabilities are used to assign labour force status. One modification is made to the probabilities. It was assumed that when someone over 53 years of age

---

1 About two-thirds of the disabled are age 55 and over.
2 Single includes divorced, widowed, and separated.

withdraws from the labour force for a year, he stays out of the labour force. In addition those who are disabled are assumed to be out of the labour force.

Self employment

The probability of being self employed (for those who work) was estimated from the Survey of Consumer Finances. The regressions contained age, education and province. The province coefficients were particularly large because of the geographic concentration of farms. The self employment variable is created at age 21, and once self employed, one is assumed to remain self employed unless he changes provinces, marries before thirty, or leaves school. In these cases self employment is reassigned, depending on the estimated probability and a random number. If one is not self employed at age 21 one could randomly become self employed at a later age, depending on the transitional probability of becoming self employed.

Unemployment

The probability of being unemployed during a year and the duration of unemployment were estimated from the Survey of Consumer Finances. The independent variables were age, education, school enrolment, province, sex, and self employment. Separate regressions were run for married men, married women, and single men and women. For those with unemployment the duration equation (weeks of unemployment) was estimated in logarithmic form. Duration was assigned in the simulation by combining the predicted duration with an error obtained from a normal distribution with a standard deviation equal to the standard error of estimate for the regression.

Earnings

The logarithm of annual earnings was estimated from the 1972 Survey of Consumer Finances. Separate regressions were run for married men, married women, single men, and single women. The independent variables were province, education, age, presence of children, school enrolment, and duration of unemployment (in step function form). The inclusion of variables which affect labour supply is justified because the number of hours worked affects earnings. The use of the log of earnings implies a log normal distribution of earnings. There is some evidence that the log normal distribution is a good approximation of the earnings distribution,[3] but when the standard error of estimate of the regression equation was applied to a log normal distribution, the resulting errors were too large. In order to more closely replicate the 1971 distributions, earnings.

3 See Blinder (1974) for a review of the literature.

were assigned using the predicted values plus an error term with a standard deviation equal to one half the standard error of estimate in the regression equations.

A particularly crucial problem for a lifetime simulation is the correlation of earnings between years. A similar problem exists with labour force participation and unemployment. Unfortunately there is little information on the year to year movements in an individual's earnings and other income items. One of the few sources of information is a panel study carried out by the Survey Research Center, University of Michigan (Benus, 1974). A study of five-year income patterns for individual families found a high degree of stability among upper income groups and found that labour income was the major source of instability, (Benus, 1974, 292-3).

The model as described so far allows for instability because of changes in age, education, marital status, children, province and duration of unemployment. Therefore, the same error term in an individual's earnings equation is applied throughout his life, with a few exceptions. An error term is generated at age 18 and again at the age of marriage if the age of marriage is less than 30. At marriage earnings of the spouse are generated given his or her characteristics.

Income other than earnings
Other income is divided into investment income and transfer income. The latter does not include payments for Old Age Security, The Canada Pension Plan, or The Quebec Pension Plan. The procedure followed was essentially the same as for earnings. The probabilities of having each of the two types of income were estimated for married couples and single individuals. The logarithm of the amount of each of these incomes was estimated separately for married couples and single individuals with each of these income types. The two income items are initially predicted at age 18, but new error terms are generated in the year of marriage if under age 30. When over age 30 the new married couple's investment and transfer income are set equal to the sum of the husband's and wife's income as single individuals. The new error term is the difference between this sum and the mean income for married couples with the same characteristics. From then on changes in income occur as predicted by the married couple's income equation. The spouse's income as a single individual must be predicted at the time of marriage. In the case of divorce the married couple's investment and transfer income is divided, and in the case of the death of the spouse the individual receives the couple's income.

Investment income was assigned to individuals based on a log normal distribution with the standard error of estimate used as the standard deviation. In the case of transfer income the standard deviation was scaled down to 75 per cent of the standard error of estimate for single individuals and 85 per cent for married couples.

THE CANADA PENSION PLAN ANALYSER

In the second part of the simulation system the contributions and benefits under the Canada Pension Plan are calculated for each of the life histories generated by the first part of the simulation system. In each year the individual's income items are updated by the rate of inflation and rate of growth of real income assumed by the program user. Contributions to the Canada Pension Plan (or the Quebec Pension Plan) are calculated for the individual and his spouse. The program allows for the user to make alternative assumptions concerning the incidence of the employer's contributions. As the contributor qualifies for benefits, whether they be for disability, the death of a spouse, or retirement, the benefits are calculated. For an individual who is still employed after age 65, the program calculates the advisability of claiming benefits before age 70 given the mortality rates and the discount rate.

The calculation of the spouse's contributions and benefits requires some special techniques. At the time of marriage the age, education, disability, employment, self employment, unemployment, earnings, and other income are predicted for the spouse, but the spouse's past contribution record is not available. In order to remedy this, whenever a marriage takes place the ratio of earnings to the year's maximum pensionable earnings, averaged over the contribution period up to the year of marriage, is stored along with the number of years in the contribution period. This information is kept in a 'marriage bank' classified by sex, education, and age of marriage. When a marriage takes place the prior contribution record of the spouse is picked up from the marriage bank, given the spouse's sex, education, and age of marriage. In effect the nearest person on the tape with the spouse's characteristics is assumed to be the spouse.

In order to calculate the present value of survivor's benefits it is necessary to know the marriage and mortality of the survivors. The program does not follow the spouse after an individual dies. Therefore, information concerning the spouse is picked up from a previous record. When someone dies whose spouse had died previously (and was eligible for survivor's benefits), the present value of the earnings-related spouse's benefits divided by the spouse's pension benefits is stored. The present value is calculated at the time the contributor died. Similarly the present value of the fraction of flat benefits received[4] and the present value of orphan's benefits are stored. When retirement or disability benefits are received in addition to survivor's benefits, both the earnings related benefit and flat benefit are adjusted. This information allows an estimate to be made of the

4 Discounting is done using the real rate of interest.

value of survivor's benefits at the time of the contributor's death. The three items are retrieved from the last person on the tape whose sex, education, and age were the same at the time of the spouse's death. The present value of the earnings ratio that is retrieved is multiplied by the deceased contributor's pension calculated at death. The flat spouse benefit for the year of death is multiplied by the present value of the flat benefits received. The sum of these two terms is the present value of the surviving spouse's benefits at the time of the death of the contributor. The present value of orphans' benefits is similarly calculated.

If a contributor dies and leaves orphans and no spouse, the value of orphan benefits cannot be obtained in the manner described above because the spouse's characteristics are not applicable. Furthermore, the aggregate value of orphans benefits would be understated if the benefits paid to true orphans (both parents deceased) were not included. Since the age pattern of children is not known, it is necessary to obtain this information from another record. Whenever a contributor dies leaving children but no spouse, the time pattern of orphans benefits is accessed from the previous family with the same number of children, sex of contributor, and age of contributor. This permits the aggregate benefits to be correctly calculated and the present value of orphan benefits to be calculated at the time the contributor dies.

The program also calculates the benefits for Quebec residents under the assumption that the Quebec Pension Plan is identical to the Canada Pension Plan. There are some differences between the two plans, but the estimates for Quebec should be approximately correct.

Old Age Security, Guaranteed Income Supplement, and Guaranteed Annual Income System (Ontario) benefits are calculated. It is assumed that the latter will be fully indexed with respect to inflation after 1975. Income taxes are calculated with the 1974 tax laws. It is assumed that the tax system is fully indexed for real growth as well as price changes after 1974. Obviously the available income information does not permit the calculation of capital gains and losses, medical expenses, etc. Exemptions for children, disability, and old age, are included, as are deductions for unemployment insurance and CPP contributions. It is assumed that the spouse with the highest earnings (or retirement income) pays taxes on the married couple's investment and transfer income. The tax rates for provinces other than Ontario are arbitrarily set equal to Ontario's. The Ontario Tax Credit is calculated under the assumption that 15 per cent of income is spent on housing.[5]

5 15.2 per cent of total expenditure was spent on shelter in 1969 (Canada, 1969, 66).

TABLE B.1

Variables created

Constant characteristics
___

SO (1) = sex
   1 = male
   2 = female
SO (2) = year of arrival in Canada (if immigrant)
SO (3) = province of birth or arrival (1. ..., 10)
   1 = Newfoundland
   2 = Prince Edward Island
   3 = Nova Scotia
   4 = New Brunswick
   5 = Quebec
   6 = Ontario
   7 = Manitoba
   8 = Saskatchewan
   9 = Alberta
  10 = British Columbia
SO (4) = year of birth (cohort identifier)
SO (5) = sex of spouse
   1 = male
   2 = female
SO (6) = year of leaving Canada (if emigrant)
SO (7) = age at death

Time-dependent characteristics
___

S (T, 1) = Marital status
   0 = single
   1 = married
   2 = widowed
   3 = divorced
S (T, 2) = age of marriage (most recent)
S (T, 3) = no. of children born
S (T, 4) = no. of dependent children
S (T, 5) = educational achievement category
   1 = elementary
   2 = some secondary
   3 = secondary graduate
   4 = some post-secondary/non-university
   5 = some post-secondary/university
   6 = post-secondary grad./non-university
   7 = university first degree (BA, BSc)
   8 = university second degree (MA, MSc)
   9 = university third degree (PhD)

TABLE B.1, continued

Variable created

Time-dependent characteristics

S (T, 6) = no. of years in post-secondary school
S (T, 7) = no. of weeks unemployed in year
    99 = out of labour force
S (T, 8) = disabled
    1 = disabled
S (T, 9) = self employed
    1 = self employed
S (T, 10) = earnings
S (T, 11) = age difference of spouse (spouse age − sample individual's age)
S (T, 12) = spouse's educational achievement
S (T, 13) = no. of weeks spouse unemployed in year
    99 = out of labour force
S (T, 14) = spouse disabled
    1 = disabled
S (T, 15) = spouse self employed
    1 = self employed
S (T, 16) = spouse's earnings
S (T, 17) = unearned income
S (T, 18) = transfer income
S (T, 19) = total income
K (T) = activity index
    1 = grade 9
    2 = grade 10
    3 = grade 11
    4 = grade 12
    5 = grade 13
    6 = CAAT 1
    7 = CAAT 2
    8 = CAAT 3
    9 = univ. 1
    10 = univ. 2
    11 = univ. 3
    12 = univ. 4
    13 = univ. 5
    14 = univ. 6
    15 = univ. 7
    16 = univ. 8
    17 = univ. 9
    18 = univ. 10
    20-22 = not in school
KS (T) = spouse activity index

TABLE B.1, continued

Variable created

Time-dependent characteristics

H (T) = province
 1 = Nfld
 2 = PEI
 3 = NS
 4 = NB
 5 = Quebec
 6 = Ont
 7 = Man
 8 = Sask
 9 = Alta
 10 = BC

Glossary

Career average plan. A unit benefit plan in which the formula which determines the pension benefit gives equal weight to the employee's earnings at any time during his working lifetime.

Contributory pension plan. A pension plan in which the employee as well as the employer is required to make contributions.

Experience deficiency. A technical term used in the provincial Pension Benefits Act to denote actuarial deficits that a private pension might suffer as a result of a divergence between its actuarial assumptions (rate of return, salary increases, and so forth) and actual experience.

Final earnings plan. A unit benefit plan in which the formula which determines the pension benefit gives sole weight to the employee's earnings for a stated period of years just prior to his retirement.

Flat benefit plan. A pension plan in which pension benefits are determined either as a fixed amount for each year of employment or as a fixed periodic amount.

Initial unfunded liability. Liabilities which result from the introduction of a private pension plan or subsequent amendments to a plan.

Level premium funding. Method of funding a private pension plan in which a constant annual premium (expressed as dollars per employee or as a percentage of payroll) is established which will, if paid in every future year, provide for all future benefits.

Locked-in. Term which indicates that contributions to a plan made on behalf of an employee cannot be withdrawn for cash, but must be in the form of a deferred annuity.

Money purchase plan. The class of pension plans in which the pension of a retiring employee is based on the accumulated amount of contributions made by or for the employee.

Non-contributory plan. A pension plan in which only the employer is required to make contributions.

Single premium funding. Method of funding a private pension plan in which the pension benefit earned or accrued for each year of plan membership is bought or funded in that year.

Unit benefit plan. The class of pension plans in which the pension benefit is determined by a formula based on the remuneration of an employee for each year or for a selected number of years of service.

Bibliography

Aaron, H. (1966) 'The social insurance paradox.' *Canadian Journal of Economics and Political Science* 32, 371-4

Almon, S. (1965) 'The distributed lag between capital appropriations and expenditures.' *Econometrica* 33, 178-96

Asimakopulos, A. (1967) 'The biological interest rate and the social utility function.' *American Economic Review* 57, 185-90

– and J.C. Weldon (1968) 'On the theory of government pension plans.' *Canadian Journal of Economics* 1, 699-717

– (1970) 'On private plans in the theory of pensions.' *Canadian Journal of Economics* 3, 223-37

Atkinson, A.B. (1970) 'National superannuation: redistribution and value for money.' *Bulletin of the Oxford University Institute of Economics and Statistics* 32, 171-85

Azariadis, C. (1975) 'Implicit contracts and underemployment equilibria.' *Journal of Political Economy* 83, 1183-202

Bankers Trust Company (1975) *1975 Study of Corporate Pension Plans* (New York: Bankers Trust Company)

Barro, R.J. (1974) 'Are government bonds net wealth.' *Journal of Political Economy* 82, 1095-117

Becker, G.S. (1964) *Human Capital: A Theoretical and Empirical Analysis with Special Reference to Education* (New York: Columbia University Press)

Benus, J. (1974) 'Income instability.' In J.N. Morgan *et al; Five Thousand American Families* University of Michigan: Survey Research Center 277-304

Bernstein, M.C. (1964) *The Future of Private Pensions* (London: Collier-Macmillan)

Bird, R. (1976) *Charging for Public Services* (Toronto: Canadian Tax Foundation)

Blinder, A.S. (1974) *Toward an Economic Theory of Income Distribution* (Cambridge: MIT Press)

Body, Z. (1976) 'Common stocks as a hedge against inflation.' *Journal of Finance* 31, 459-70

Bossons, J.D. (1974) 'Indexing financial instruments for inflation.' *Canadian Tax Journal* 22, 107-17

Branch, B. (1974) 'Common stock performance and inflation: an international comparison.' *Journal of Business* 47, 48-52

Branson, W.H. (1972) *Macroeconomic Theory and Policy* (New York: Harper and Row)

Brittain, J.A. (1972) *The Payroll Tax for Social Security* (Washington, DC: The Brookings Institution)

Browning, E.K. (1973) 'Social insurance and intergenerational transfers.' *Journal of Law and Economics* 16, 215-37

– (1975) 'Labor supply distortions of social security.' *Southern Economic Journal* 42, 243-52

Bryden, K. (1974) *Old Age Pensions and Policy Making in Canada* (Montreal: McGill-Queens University Press)

Cagan, P. (1965) *The Effect of Pension Plans on Aggregate Saving: Evidence From a Sample Survey* (New York: Columbia University Press, 1965)

– (1974) 'Common stock values and inflation – the historical record of many countries.' In *National Bureau Report Supplement* (New York: National Bureau of Economic Research)

Calvert, G.N. (1977) *Pensions and Survival* (Toronto: Financial Post Books)

Canada (1969) Statistics Canada, *Family Expenditure in Canada, 1969,* vol. 1

– (1972a) Statistics Canada, *Pension Plans in Canada 1970*

– (1972b) Statistics Canada, *Estimated Participation Rates in Canadian Education, 1968-1969*

– (1973a) Statistics Canada, *Vital Statistics*

– (1973b) Department of Insurance, *Canada Pension Plan Statutory Actuarial Report Number 3*

– (1973c) Statistics Canada, *Trusteed Pension Plans Financial Statistics*

– (1974a) Statistics Canada, *Population Projections for Canada and the Provinces 1972-2000*

– (1974b) Canada Pension Plan, *Statistical Bulletin* 6, no. 4

– (1974c) Statistics Canada, *1971 Census of Canada,* vol. I, part 5

– (1974d) Statistics Canada, *1971 Census of Canada, Population: Internal Migration,* vol. 1, part 2

- (1975a) *Canadian Statistical Review*
- (1975b) Advisory Committee of the Canada Pension Plan, *The Rate of Return on the Investment Fund of the Canada Pension Plan.*
- (1975c) Department of Manpower and Immigration, *Immigration Statistics*
- (1976), Office of the Minister of National Health and Welfare, News Release, 4 Feb.

Canadian Institute of Actuaries (1975) 'Submission to the conference of the Canadian Association of Pension Supervisory Authorities.' March

Canadian Labour Congress (1975) 'Discussion Paper.' Presented at the first conference of the Canadian Association of Pension Supervisory Authorities

Carr, J. and L.B. Smith (1972) 'Money supply, interest rates and the yield curve.' *Journal of Money, Credit and Banking* 4, 582-94

Carr, J., J.E. Pesando, and L.B. Smith (1976) 'Tax effects, price expectations and the nominal rate of interest.' *Economic Inquiry* 14, 259-69

Carroll, J.J. (1960) *Alternative Methods of Financing Old-Age Survivors and Disability Insurance* (Ann Arbor: University of Michigan, Institute of Public Administration)

CCH Canadian (1976) *Canadian Employment Benefits and Pension Guide Reports* (Don Mills, CCH Canadian)

Darby, M.R. (1975) 'The financial and tax effects of monetary policy on interest rates.' *Economy Inquiry* 12, 266-76

DeMenil, G. and S.S. Bhalla (1975) 'Direct measurement of popular price expectations.' *American Economic Review* 65, 169-80

Denton, F.T. and B.G. Spencer (1975) 'The demographic element in the burden of old age pensions.' Working paper 75-02 (McMaster University: Department of Economics)

Deutsch, A. (1968) *Income Redistribution Through Canadian Federal Family Allowances and Old Age Benefits.* Queen's University Papers on Taxation and Public Finance, no. 4 (Toronto: Canadian Tax Foundation)

- (1975) 'Inflation and guaranteed formula pension plans.' *Canadian Journal of Economics* 8, 447-8

Dobell, A.R. and M.A. Cohen (1975) 'Synthetic longitudinal sampling and its application to public policy analysis.' Mimeo

Fama, E.F. (1970) 'Efficient capital markets: a review of theory and empirical work.' *Journal of Finance* 25, 383-417

- *et al.* (1969) 'The adjustment of stock prices to new information.' *International Economic Review* 10, 1-21

Feldstein, M. (1974a) 'Social security induced retirement and aggregate capital accumulation.' *Journal of Political Economy* 82, 905-26

- (1974b) 'The optimal financing of social security.' Discussion paper no. 388 (Harvard Institute of Economic Research)

- (1974c) 'Financing in the evaluation of public expenditure.' In W. Smith *et al.*, eds., *Essays in Public Finance and Stabilization Policy* (Amsterdam: North Holland)
- (1974d) 'The incidence of the social security payroll tax: comment.' *American Economic Review* 62, 735-8
- (1976a) 'Social security and saving: the extended life cycle theory.' *American Economic Review* 66, 77-86
- (1976b) 'Perceived wealth in bonds and social security: a comment.' *Journal of Political Economy* 84, 331-6
- and O. Eckstein (1970) 'The fundamental determinants of the interest rate.' *Review of Economics and Statistics* 52, 363-75

Fisher, I. (1930) *The Theory of Interest* (New York: Macmillan)

Fischer, S. (1975) 'The demand for index bonds.' *Journal of Political Economy* 83, 509-34

Foot, D. (1975) 'Provincial public finances in Ontario' (University of Toronto: Institute for Policy Analysis)

Gibson, W.E. (1972) 'Interest rates and inflationary expectations: new evidence.' *American Economic Review* 62, 854-65

Giersch, H. *et al.* (1974) *Essays on Inflation and Indexation* (Washington, DC: Domestic Affairs)

Ganasekeran, K.S. (1970) 'Migration projections for Canada 1969-1984.' Analytical and Technical Memorandum no. 6., Dominion Bureau of Statistics

Gordon, D.F. 'A neo-classical theory of Keynesian unemployment.' *Economic Inquiry* 12, 431-59

Habib, J. and R. Lerman (1976) 'Equity and the social insurance paradox.' Discussion paper no. 3-76 (Jerusalem: Brookdale Institute)

Hamming. R.W. (1962) *Numerical Methods for Scientists and Engineers* (New York: McGraw-Hill)

Harvey, E.C. (1965) 'Social Security taxes – regressive or progressive? *National Tax Journal* XVIII, 408-14

Hicks, J.R. (1946) *Value and Capital* (Oxford: Oxford University Press)

Hildreth, C. and J.Y. Lu (1960) *Demand Relations with Autocorrelated Disturbances.* Technical bulletin no. 276 (Michigan State University)

Ibbotson, R.G. and R.A. Sinquefield (1975) 'Stocks, bonds, bills and inflation: year-by-year historical returns (1926-1974).' *Journal of Business* 49, 11-47

Institute for Policy Analysis (1975) 'Canadian long-term outlook' (University of Toronto: Institute for Policy Analysis)

Jenkins, G. (1972) 'Analysis of rates of return from capital in Canada.' Unpublished PhD Dissertation (University of Chicago)

Jenkins, G.P. and H.B.F. Lim (1973) 'The role of Canadian and United States monetary policy in the determination of interest rates in Canada.' Discussion paper no. 326 (Harvard Institute of Economic Research)

Kane, E.J. and B.G. Malkiel (1976) 'Autoregressive and nonautoregressive elements in cross-section forecasts of inflation.' *Econometrica* 44, 1-16

Lerner, A.P. (1959) 'Consumption-loan interest and money.' *Journal of Political Economy* 67, 512-18

Life Underwriters Association of Canada (1975) 'Memorandum re: private pension plan legislation.' Brief submitted to the Canadian Association of Pension Supervisory Authorities (March 1975)

Lintner, J. (1973) 'Inflation and common stock prices in a cyclical context.' In National Bureau of Economic Research, *53rd Annual Report,* 23-36

– (1975) 'inflation and security returns.' *Journal of Finance* 30, 259-80

MacIntosh, R.M. (1976) 'The great pension fund robbery.' *Canadian Public Policy* 2, 256-62

Modigliani, F. and R. Shiller (1973) 'Inflation, rational expectations and the term structure of interest rates.' *Economica* 40, 315-35

Munnell, A. (1974) *The Effect of Social Security on Personal Saving* (Cambridge: Ballinger Publishing Co.)

Muth, J.F. (1961) 'Rational expectations and the theory of price movements.' *Econometrica* 29, 315-35

Nelson, C.R. (1976) 'Inflation and the rates of return on common stocks.' *Journal of Finance* 31, 471-83

Ontario (1961) Committee on Portable Pensions, *Second Report*

– (1972) Pension Commission of Ontario, 'A proposal to amend the Pension Benefits Act of Ontario'

– (1974) *Budget Statements*

– (1975a) *Ontario Budget*

– (1975b) Pension Commission of Ontario, 'Preliminary report of the funded status of certain pension plans registered with the Pension Commission of Ontario' (18 Aug. 1975)

– (1976) Ministry of Treasury, Economics and Intergovernmental Affairs, 'Review of issues in financing the Canada Pension Plan'

Ozawa, M.N. (1974) 'Individual equity versus social adequacy in federal old-age insurance,' *Social Service Review* 48, 24-38

Pesando, J.E. (1974) 'The supply of money and common stock prices: further observations on the econometric evidence.' *Journal of Finance* 29, 909-21

– (1975a) 'Determinants of term premiums in the market for United States Treasury bills.' *Journal of Finance* 30, 1317-27

– (1975b) 'The impact of the conversion loan on the term structure of interest rates in Canada: some additional evidence.' *Canadian Journal of Economics* 8, 281-88
– (1975c) 'A note on the rationality of the Livingston price expectations.' *Journal of Political Economy* 83, 849-58
– (1976) 'Alternative models of the determination of nominal interest rates: the Canadian evidence.' *Journal of Money, Credit and Banking* 8, 209-18
– (1977) *The Impact of Inflation on Financial Markets in Canada* (Montreal: C.D. Howe Research Institute)
– and J.A. Sawyer (1975) 'A note on price expectations and wage "catch-up".' Working paper no. 7507 (University of Toronto: Institute for Policy Analysis)
Prest, A.R. (1970) 'Some redistributional aspects of the national superannuation fund.' *The Three Banks Review* 86, 3-22
Pyle, D.H. (1972) 'Observed price expectations and interest rates.' *Review of Economics and Statistics* 54, 275-80
Rea, S.A. (1974a) 'Investment in human capital and income maintenance programs." Working paper no. 7404 (University of Toronto: Institute for Policy Analysis)
– (1974b) 'Trade-offs between alternative income maintenance programs.' In US Joint Economic Committee, *Studies in Public Welfare,* no. 13, 33-63
Rutledge, J. (1974a) *A Monetarist Model of Inflationary Expectations* (Lexington: Lexington Books)
Samuelson, P.A. (1958) 'An exact consumption-loan model of interest with or without the social contrivance of money.' *Journal of Political Economy* 66, 467-82
Samuelson, P.A. (1959) 'Consumption-loan interest and money: reply.' *Journal of Political Economy* 67, 518-22
Sargent, T.J. (1971) 'A note on the 'accelerationist' controversy.' *Journal of Money, Credit and Banking* 3, 721-5
– (1972) 'Rational expectations and the term structure of interest rates.' *Journal of Money, Credit and Banking* 4, 74-97
Schmidt, P. and R.N. Waud (1973) 'The almon lag debate and the monetary versus fiscal policy debate.' *Journal of the American Statistical Association* 68, 11-19
Schiller, B.R. and R.D. Weiss (1977) 'Pensions and wages: a test for equalizing difference.' University of Maryland, January 1977
Schulz, J. *et al.* (1974) *Providing Adequate Retirement Income* (Hanover: University Press of New England)

Simeon, R. (1972) *Federal-Provincial Diplomacy: The Making of Recent Policy in Canada* (Toronto: University of Toronto Press)

Taussig, M.K. (1975) 'The social security retirement program and welfare reform.' In I. Lurie, ed., *Integrating Income Maintenance Programs* (New York: Academic Press)

Thurow, L.C. (1969) *Poverty and Discrimination* (Washington, DC: Brookings Institution)

Upton, C. (1975) 'Review of *The Effect of Social Security on Personal Saving* by Alicia Munnell.' *Journal of Political Economy* 83, 1090-2

US Congress (1973) Joint Economic Committee, *The Labor Market Impacts of the Private Retirement System*

US Congress (1974) *Employee Retirement Income Security Act of 1974*

Van Praag, B. and G. Poeth (1975) 'The introduction of an old-age pension in a growing economy.' *Journal of Public Economics* 4, 87-100

Yohe, W.P. and D.S. Karnosky (1969) 'Interest rates and price level changes.' Federal Reserve Bank of St Louis, *Review* 51, 19-36